Classic Eateries

OF THE

ARKANSAS DELTA

Classic Eateries

OF THE

ARKANSAS DELTA

KAT ROBINSON

Photography by
GRAV WELDON

AMERICAN PALATE

Published by American Palate
A Division of The History Press
Charleston, SC 29403
www.historypress.net

Front cover images (clockwise from upper left): Rustic Inn, Blytheville (historic postcard); Dog n Suds, Paragould (Grav Weldon); Josie's at the Lockhouse, Batesville (Kat Robinson); Trio Club, Pine Bluff (historic photograph); Order-Matic at Burger Shack, Helena–West Helena (Kat Robinson); Rhoda's Famous Hot Tamales, Lake Village (Grav Weldon).

Back cover images: The Browns with Elvis Presley at the Trio Club, Pine Bluff (courtesy Maxine Brown); Hamburger Station, Paragould (Grav Weldon); tamales at Rhoda's Famous Hot Tamales, Lake Village (Grav Weldon).

First published 2014

Manufactured in the United States

ISBN 978.1.62619.756.5

Library of Congress CIP data applied for.

Notice: The information in this book is true and complete to the best of our knowledge. It is offered without guarantee on the part of the author or The History Press. The author and The History Press disclaim all liability in connection with the use of this book.

For more information on Arkansas foodways, restaurants and itineraries, please visit TieDyeTravels.com.

To Neale and April Carter, and to Leif Hassell
My Greek chorus

And to Kim Williams
The voice of the Arkansas Delta

CONTENTS

Contents

FOREWORD

I'm sitting down to write this foreword on the day after my favorite event of the summer—the Grady Fish Fry in the Hardin pecan grove in Grady in Lincoln County.

For the fifty-ninth time, the Grady Lions Club put on an event that drew people from all over southeast Arkansas, not to mention the fact that it attracted seemingly every politician in the state. It was hot and humid, in contrast to what has been an unseasonably cool summer here in Arkansas, but the crowd seemed bigger than it has been in recent years. The fried catfish, fries, hushpuppies and sliced watermelon were as good as ever. And there in the thick of things, taking photos and talking to people, was Kat Robinson. Kat seems to be everywhere when it comes to chronicling the state's food culture.

Like me, Kat doesn't hail from the Arkansas Delta. Also like me, she has an affinity for this historic part of Arkansas, which has been losing population since at least 1950. There's something that captures your soul when driving those back roads of the Arkansas Delta, and often the attraction is food.

My favorite barbecue in Arkansas? Craig's in DeValls Bluff. My favorite catfish in Arkansas? Murry's, near Hazen. My favorite tamales in Arkansas? Rhoda's in Lake Village. My favorite plate lunch in Arkansas? The Pickens Commissary in Pickens, which is just south of Dumas. My favorite place to hang out in a restaurant's back room and swap tales with hunting buddies? Gene's in Brinkley. I said my favorite summer event is the Grady Fish Fry, so my favorite winter event? The Slovak Oyster Supper in southern Prairie County.

All of these places are in east Arkansas. And I'm from southwest Arkansas, though I have roots in the east, since my mother grew up along the lower White River in Des Arc. When it comes to eating, give me the Delta. Give me a lunch at Rhoda's Famous Hot Tamales, where Rhoda Adams has been turning out Delta-style tamales for almost four decades. Her husband's aunt asked her to try making tamales, and the rest is history. Rhoda is the mother of fifteen children, only eleven of whom survived to adulthood. She has almost sixty grandchildren and great-grandchildren, some of whom she has never met. Business executives have been known to fly private jets down from Little Rock just to have lunch with Rhoda and then take several dozen tamales home.

Give me a Friday night supper of catfish cooked by Stanley Young at Murry's on U.S. Highway 70 between Hazen and Carlisle. I began patronizing the original Murry's in DeValls Bluff when I was a child. My grandparents lived in Des Arc, and we would often make the short road trip from the Prairie County seat in the north to the Prairie County seat in the south in order to consume mounds of catfish at Murry's or barbecue at Craig's.

When I was in my twenties, there were times when I would load up the car with hungry friends for a trip to DeValls Bluff. We would have a pork sandwich at Craig's (with medium sauce, since the hot sauce is a bit too hot for my taste) for an appetizer and then drive over to Murry's for catfish. I miss that rabbit warren of trailers that housed the original location, though I always had the feeling when eating there that a grease fire in the kitchen would quickly incinerate us all. While the current location doesn't have the ambiance of the old place, the food is as good as ever, maybe better. And Becky Young is the best hostess you'll find anywhere.

Give me a plate of barbecue at any number of places in the Delta, the strongest barbecue area of a good barbecue state. The barbecue is pork here (beef has crept over from Texas into parts of southwest Arkansas), though the sauces vary from place to place. At Craig's, you'll walk into the ramshackle building and immediately be asked if you want your barbecue sauce mild, medium or hot. The crowd is a mixture of locals, hunters from Little Rock and Memphis when it's duck season and those who were wise enough to get off crowded Interstate 40 and find their way to DeValls Bluff.

In Marianna, meanwhile, Jones' Bar-B-Q Diner, the winner of the James Beard Foundation's American Classics Award, can be found in an old house in a residential area. Jones' has been around since at least the early 1900s. While it's hard to determine the exact year it opened, there are some historians who believe it's the oldest continuously operated black-owned restaurant in the South.

Up in the far northeast part of the state, you'll find five or six good barbecue joints in Blytheville, a fact that led me to proclaim it the Barbecue Capital of Arkansas.

Yes, the Delta is a place apart. To me, the Grady Fish Fry represents all that is good about the Delta—a sense of history, community, continuity and place. Good friends, good food and helping others.

I checked my old calendars and was able to determine that this was the eighteenth time in the past nineteen years that I've been in Grady on the third Thursday in August. The only fish fry I missed during that stretch was a decade ago. I was Governor Mike Huckabee's representative on the board of the Delta Regional Authority (DRA) at the time, and we were interviewing candidates in a Memphis hotel that day for the job of DRA chief operating officer.

The fish fry is like something out of a movie about the South—the convicts in their prison whites waiting tables, the prison band playing, the politicians making the rounds. If you have any doubt that the South still lives, all you have to do is show up at Ned Hardin's pecan grove on the third Thursday night in August one year, and all doubts will be erased. They start serving the fish at 4:00 p.m. and stop at 8:00 p.m. In between, hundreds of people make their way through the lines, loading their paper plates and watching the amazing hushpuppy machine (constructed years ago from salvaged farm equipment) drop batter into the hot grease, two hushpuppies at a time.

Kat has done a real service by capturing so many Delta restaurants, events and traditions, many of which likely won't exist a decade from now. The economic trends, unfortunately, are working against these places. I see nothing on the horizon that leads me to believe that the population shift in this state from the east and the south to the north and the west will slow anytime soon. Most Delta counties have been losing population since the end of World War II, when the mechanization of agriculture meant that thousands of sharecroppers and tenant farmers were no longer required. Monroe County, which includes Brinkley and Clarendon, lost a larger percentage of its population between the 2000 census and the 2010 census than any county in Arkansas—20.5 percent. This trend is not confined to the Arkansas Delta, mind you. Rural America now accounts for just 16.0 percent of the nation's population.

Mark Mather of the Population Reference Bureau put it this way: "Some of the most isolated rural areas face a major uphill battle, with a broad area of the country emptying out. Many rural areas can't attract workers because there aren't any jobs, and businesses won't relocate there because there aren't enough qualified workers. So they are caught in a downward spiral."

In his 1997 book *Rising Tide*, which chronicles the Great Flood of 1927 of the Mississippi River, author John Barry closes with rumination on societal changes: "A society does not change in sudden jumps. Rather, it moves in multiple small steps along a broad front. Most of these steps are parallel if not quite simultaneous; some advance farther than others, and some even move in an opposite direction. The movement rather resembles that of an amoeba, with one part of the body extending itself outward, then another, even while the main body stays back, until enough of the mass has shifted to move the entire body."

So it is in the Delta of east Arkansas. There have been no sudden leaps forward following decades of economic decline, no giant automobile assembly plants, no ethanol boom, no discovery of vast oil and gas reserves. But there are many talented people, including those who run the region's restaurants, who are taking those "multiple small steps" forward, hoping that the steps will result in a better life for the people who live in this historic, culturally rich part of the state.

Delta residents are among the most resilient people in our country. The Delta experienced the Civil War, Reconstruction, yellow fever and other epidemics. Then came the Great Flood of 1927. Just as the region was beginning to recover from the flood, the Great Depression began in 1929. Another flood covered the region in 1937. Much of the rest of the nation began to prosper again in the years immediately following World War II. Thanks to the GI Bill, thousands of veterans became the first members of their families to attend college. Following college, they married, bought homes and purchased automobiles. The steel industry boomed. The automobile industry also prospered. In the Delta, though, the mechanization of cotton farming and the evils of segregation drove thousands of people—African Americans and poor whites—out of the state. Men and women who had once worked as tenants on the plantations of east Arkansas were working, in the years after World War II, in steel mills and automobile factories in places such as Detroit, Cleveland and Chicago.

One only has to drive through rural east Arkansas during the Christmas holidays to see the automobile license plates in the driveways from Illinois, Michigan and even California. These are the children and grandchildren of people who left their native Arkansas in search of better opportunities.

During the past decade, the Delta has done a better job of attracting those drawn to heritage tourism. Blues tourists come to the region to pay homage to their blues heroes, eat pork barbecue and then head home. For far too many of those who actually live in the region, though, the blues are all too real. If they have a job, the chances are that their wages are low. Too often, their health is poor and the education their children receive is not up to par.

But the Delta matters. The best-known American music has its roots in the region. The Delta counties on both sides of the Mississippi River have supplied our nation with many of its finest statesmen, writers and chefs. And there's the unique ethnic mix. In addition to the African American culture, there are the Italians who came to the region as sharecroppers and the Jews who settled along the Mississippi River as merchants. The Chinese came to build railroads and sometimes stayed to run businesses. Across the Delta, one can still find grocery stores with names such as Fong and Wong. The Lebanese and Syrian merchants added to this fascinating cultural stew.

The sharecropping era, when hundreds of people flocked to Delta crossroads communities each Saturday night, ended long ago. For many Arkansawyers with roots in the region, the Delta is no longer the place they call home. It's instead a charming place to hunt, fish, experience the blues and eat out before returning home to Little Rock, Fayetteville, Fort Smith or Texarkana. We cannot allow this part of our state to become nothing more than a hauntingly beautiful but increasingly deserted museum piece. The Arkansas Delta and the gracious people who still call it home deserve better than that. Thanks to my friend Kat Robinson for capturing an important part of their story.

REX NELSON
August 22, 2014

HOW TO USE THIS BOOK

I never, in my wildest imagination, could have conjured the usage derived by readers of *Arkansas Pie: A Delicious Slice of the Natural State* and *Classic Eateries of the Ozarks and Arkansas River Valley*. For me, a book is to be savored from cover to cover. The idea of taking small bites wasn't apparent.

However, that's how certain readers have taken these tomes, stashing them away in glove compartments, ready to access them in any of the cities within the book's regional coverage. The handy index in the back makes it easy to search by city for restaurants along the route.

This book is set up for your reading pleasure. Consume it from front to back if you wish, or utilize it as a roadmap to culinary adventures. The listings within have been carefully laid out along the Arkansas Delta's roadways, highways, byways and passages. It is possible to reach every location in the order recorded within; however, I'd suggest giving yourself weeks to accomplish this trick. After all, there are few who can sustain dining repeatedly when the number of eateries surpasses one hundred.

Consider this guide a "Choose Your Own Adventure," whether in your vehicle or your recliner, and if you get hung up or a restaurant is closed, feel free to message me for another recommendation. After all, Arkansas has so many great restaurants to offer.

One more thing: There are many classic restaurants in this region, and though months of diligent research were conducted, I know there are likely a handful of great eateries I missed. That's the nature of a book like this. I hope I've completed it to serve you best.

ACKNOWLEDGEMENTS

This book wouldn't have been possible without the continued and sustained support of numerous individuals, including David Backlin, Talya Tate Boerner, Mark Christ, Norwood Creech, Eric Francis, Susan Gallion, Cindy Grisham, Rex Nelson, Cindy Smith, Kim Williams, the Arkansas Highway and Transportation Department, the Arkansas History Commission, the Butler Center for Arkansas Studies, the Central Arkansas Library System, the *Encyclopedia of Arkansas History and Culture*, the Delta Cultural Center, the Helena Museum of Phillips County, the Historic Arkansas Museum, the Museum of the Arkansas Grand Prairie, the Southern Food and Beverage Museum, the Southern Foodways Alliance, the Southern Tenant Farmers Museum, the Writers' Colony at Dairy Hollow and Arkansas State University's Heritage Sites program.

Additional thanks go to the many restaurant owners, managers, waitstaff, cooks and chefs who contributed to this effort.

Part One

THE LOWER DELTA

1

THE GREAT RIVER ROAD, SOUTH

JONES' BAR-B-Q DINER, MARIANNA

No one knows just how old Jones' Bar-B-Q Diner is, but Mr. Harold Jones says the recipe goes back 150 years or more. His grandfather and uncle made and sold barbecue from the same recipe he uses today. Everyone agrees that the place was open in 1910, so we can at least surmise that the Marianna staple is past the century mark.

Harold Jones's grandfather used to go downtown on Saturdays and sell barbecued pork from a washtub, what folks called the Hole in the Ground. On Fridays, he and Jones's grandmother would sell it out the kitchen door of their home on the corner of California and Florida Streets.

Jones himself has been in the business since 1968, in what started as a little one-story building on Louisiana Street. The flat-topped building was constructed in 1964. He says, "I was fourteen years old when they let me outta school when there was too much to cook. Me and my brother got out of school to do it." Over the years, add-ons were built, including a second story where Jones sleeps when he's not home with his wife, Betty.

Every day he gets up and opens at 6:00 a.m. Every day it's all gone before the lunch hour is over. Sometimes it's gone by 11:00 a.m., depending on who's come to town. "Back in May, there were judges who came down to Memphis, to the big cookoff up there, and they'd ask," Mr. Harold told me, "'Where's the best barbecue around here?' And these guys, these guys who were cooking off, they'd say, 'You have to go down to Marianna,' and they came.

"The governor, he sent me an autographed photograph," he continued, waving his hand toward the wall by the guest book, where a smiling image of Arkansas governor Mike Beebe looks out into the diner. "Day he came in here, he brought a whole lot of people. They packed in like sardines, but everyone was havin' a good time."

Every day it's still three dollars a sandwich, six dollars a pound. Sandwiches are made on Sunbeam white bread, always the same—lay down the plate or aluminum foil, put down a slice, heap a mound of pork on it, drizzle on the thin sauce, dollop with sweet coleslaw, top with another slice and wrap. When there's not someone waiting, Jones keeps making them. He wraps each one in foil and deposits it in an electric roaster.

Butts—pork butts, that is—are put on a wire rack in a makeshift pit about eight by sixteen feet. The rack looks just like the inside of an old-style box-spring mattress. The coals come from a fireplace that is a half century old or better; hickory and oak burned down until they gleam red on black from the gray ashes shoveled into the pit. That's the only heat the meat will get—the slow heat from hot wood and hot charcoal. A plywood cover on a pulley goes down and the meat smokes.

There's not much more to it than that, except the sauce. Jones doesn't let anyone know the family secret, not even his wife. It's stored in a variety of vessels—gallon jugs formerly used for other items along the back of the kitchen and sixteen-ounce water bottles for handing out with big meat orders.

Out in the dining area, there's a guest book. It's a little yellowed, but it's still somewhat new; the smoke probably colors it a bit. Flip the pages, and you'll see a random smattering of places beside the names—Stuttgart, Arkansas, right before London; New York City; Yemen; Alaska; Memphis; San Francisco; Beirut, Lebanon; Israel; and even Japan—a collection of handwritten testaments from travelers the world over who have come to this little two-top diner that's not even on the main highway of a small town in the Arkansas Delta.

We got into town at 10:20 a.m. on a Saturday in July, sure the barbecue was already gone. I could already smell the place before I turned off Alabama Street.

Grav had never been, but I had—several times, in fact—which is only equaled in strangeness by the fact that I can't eat what Mr. Jones sells. I'm allergic to pork. Still, I'd been selling the idea of the place to my photographer for a few days, and when we got out of the car, I knew the sale was closed.

Harold Jones waits at the window for orders inside Jones' Barbecue Diner in Marianna. His James Beard American Classic award hangs above. *Graw Weldon.*

Grav started popping around shooting the exterior with an urgency of needing to taste what he was smelling. I've rarely seen that in humans—it's usually reserved for cats hearing the sound of an electric can opener.

It's not that I haven't experienced the sauce. The day *Arkansas Pie: A Delicious Slice of the Natural State* came out, Kim Williams brought up Mr. Jones's good meat. It was Second Friday Art Night in downtown Little Rock, and the Historic Arkansas Museum (hosting not just my signing but another and debuting a Delta art show) was feeding folks his barbecue and fried pies in celebration. Kim also brought along a couple whole smoked chickens, and Grav and I had our share bare-fingered in the upstairs catering kitchen with a little squirt of sauce here and there, quickly consuming what we could before folks started showing up. It was as fulfilling as any fine dining experience.

When we got inside, Grav was full of questions—which was good, since Mr. Harold (I've just started to think of him that way, since that's how Kim refers to him) is quick to answer them. Recognizing the guy with the camera in hand as a newcomer, he stepped out of the kitchen and started talking. He reached up with one hand and plucked a box off the wall above the kitchen window, a black shadowbox frame with a ribbon and a medal in it.

It was his James Beard award. That's right, the only place in Arkansas to actually receive the Oscar of restaurants is a little, white two-story barbecue shack in the Delta. Mr. Harold used to just pull it out and hand it to folks and show it off before Kim got him the box.

Before the spring of 2012, no one could imagine such an august award for the place. They just knew the barbecue was good, cheap and consistent. Since the nomination, Mr. Harold has been profiled by *CBS Sunday Morning*, talked with reporters from every variety of press and broadcast and welcomed visitors from Paris, London and Japan. It's not uncommon for journalists and bloggers to pop in unannounced. He takes it all in stride.

Here he was answering questions he must have answered thousands of times by now, from yet another guy with a camera. I just took notes and watched.

After showing off the medal and replacing it on the wall, Mr. Harold stepped back into the kitchen, answering even more questions along the way. He stepped back to the counter and proceeded to make another sandwich—foil, bread, 'cue, sauce, coleslaw, bread, wrap, roaster. He began another—foil, bread, 'cue, sauce, coleslaw, bread, wrap, roaster, as automatic as you please.

When I finally got a chance to get a word in edgewise, I handed Mr. Harold a five-dollar bill and asked if he'd make one for Grav. He handed me change and a sandwich and nodded to the refrigerator in the dining room and said, "Get that boy a Coke." I did, and by the time I turned around Grav had half-inhaled the sandwich. I just saw a grown man fall in love. It was a beautiful thing.

I heard Grav say something he doesn't usually say. He will tell someone their food is the best in the area, or one of the best things he's eaten that day, but rarely will he utter words like these: "Your barbecue is about the best I have ever had."

His sandwich gone, he wiped his hands, grabbed the camera and looked for more to shoot. He had Mr. Harold hold the medal and shot him, had him stand in the kitchen and peer out the window and shot him again. All the time, Mr. Harold continued the story, one told many times but always with pride.

A young woman opened the door and peered in. She noticed me standing there, and Grav and the big camera, and hesitated.

"Can I help you, young lady?" Mr. Harold called out to her.

"I wan' a sannich," she called back, finally sliding in and closing the door behind her.

"Wi' slaw or wi' out?"

"Wi'."

I could see him making the sandwich the entire bit of conversation, not taking his eyes off her until he went to squirt on the sauce. He paused a bare second to hear whether she wanted the slaw, and when she answered, the slaw plopped down on the meat and the bread was slid on over. It didn't take him but a second to wrap the sandwich and pass it out of the kitchen. She handed him her three dollars in the same motion and was back out the door.

He led us through the kitchen to the back of the building to see where the barbecue is smoked. Being now lunchtime on a Saturday, the smoking had ended for the day. Three younger men were sitting around on chairs and an old van bench watching a white television set showing—I kid you not—*It's a Wonderful Life*. One of the guys got up and showed us the pit. I marveled at the interior of the back screened-in section. Decades of smoke had turned the ceiling a deep-charred black, but not just the ceiling—the walls were dark and stunk of sweat and salt. A windowpane was stained with brownish-red flamelike flanges where the smoke had intruded. And it smelled. It smelled like I hope heaven smells.

Grav asked the guy showing off the pit, "So, do you like this barbecue?"

He chuckled. "I've eaten so many over the years, sometimes I might eat one, sometimes I might not."

Back in the restaurant itself, we were making our farewells when one of the regulars came in. He grinned and offered testament himself: "I was telling him the other day I ate his father's barbecue, and every time someone comes in with a camera, he goes and raises the prices!" Both men laughed; the prices haven't gone up in a long time, and Mr. Harold Jones isn't giving any indication that they'll change any time soon.

MARIANNA AT THE CROSSROADS

Marianna lies at the crux of two great national byways—Crowley's Ridge Parkway, which goes north up and along the ridge that divides the Arkansas Delta in half; and the Great River Road, which hopscotches a number of state highways and country roads here and passes through nine states on either side of the Mississippi. There aren't many restaurants in Marianna these days, just a few little spots here and there. But back in the 1920s, it was where Bulgarian immigrant George Petkoff and Macedonian native Tanas Tripp Traicoff started the National Baking Company, which would later move to Helena and become the Royal Baking Company. Marianna's status as a crossroads in the heart of the Delta made it a good jumping-off point for the research on this book, not just because of Mr. Jones, but also because of the many highways that spiderweb out from the hub, just off the Mississippi River.

Where to go first? Grav and I decided to make our way south on Arkansas Highway 1 to see what we might find. Of course, the first classic restaurant on this path happened to be Alton Brown's only Great River Road stop in Arkansas, at a little dairy diner that never expected the attention.

RAY'S DAIRY MAID, BARTON

How long has Ray's Dairy Maid been around? Long enough for Ray to not be anymore, and long enough for the place to have well established itself as a standout must-stop on the trek to Helena–West Helena each year for the King Biscuit Blues Festival. Locals recall rolling in from Marianna and up from as far as DeWitt and farther to have a bite. Some even remember a similar restaurant, Ray's Kool Freeze, in nearby Marvell.

"Nana" Deane Cavette at her restaurant, Ray's Dairy Maid in Barton. *Kat Robinson.*

Today, Deane Cavette, a second mother to many of those who come by, runs the place. Though *Frommer's* recently stated she's been serving food there for more than fifty years, I don't believe that for a second. Deane is a lot of things, but ancient she isn't. She has an energy to her that glows from within.

Some of the confusion over when she started serving might come from how Deane started out. She began working at the family restaurant, the aforementioned Ray's Kool Freeze (opened in 1955), when she was fourteen. Back in those days, some Arkansas restaurants were still segregated, with split dining rooms. Deane told me, with an ounce of shame, that this was the case at the Cavette family–run restaurant. It was a different time, we both agreed.

Ray's Dairy Maid established itself as the local spot for Barton teenagers and families way back in the 1950s. When it came up for sale in the 1970s, Deane bought it and kept the name.

I talked about Ray's Dairy Maid in the pie book; I've dreamed of it any time pecans come to mind. More than once, I've found a reason to divert my travels from wherever I was planning to go to sweep by, duck into the dining room to check the pie case and then order at the window. In fact, on this particular trip through the Delta, despite being quite full from Pasquale's Tamales (which I'll tell you about in a few pages), we stopped in, parking at the business next door because there were more than three dozen cars in the lot. Grav shot the interior, where there wasn't a single spare table, and I counted the slices. And then, greedy person I am, I ordered both of the slices left of the pecan coconut pie.

The pie didn't make it back to Little Rock. In fact, it didn't even make it to the fork, with each of us swiping chunks off our slices with our fingers from their white clamshell boxes as we headed down the highway.

Pie is not all Ray's Dairy Maid serves, though, if you'd believe the press (and you might because of that *Feasting on Asphalt* appearance), it might as well be. Ray's is also a true and dedicated drive-in, with good burgers and plate lunches and a killer breakfast. The shakes are gobstoppingly good: thick and packed with just enough extra chocolate or fruit in them to make you shut up and enjoy the ride when you're headed down the road, which we did.

HELENA–WEST HELENA

Phillips County is named after Sylvanus Phillips, who first arrived on the land in 1797. It was carved out of a Spanish land grant in 1820 and given his name. The town of Helena, incorporated and named in 1832, bears the name of his daughter, who had died at the age of fifteen.

The port town was founded seven and a half miles south of where the Saint Francis River converges with the Mississippi, at the tail end of Crowley's Ridge. It became the largest Arkansas town along the big river before the Civil War. In 1862, a Union military unit under the command of Brigadier General Samuel Ryan Curtis took control of the city and constructed a fort. Confederate forces tried to storm the garrison on July 4, 1863, but were pushed back and defeated. You can visit several Civil War sites in the town today, including the garrison at Fort Curtis.

Before and after the war, Helena served as the main stopover point between Memphis and Vicksburg on the river. Cotton was king, and the port saw its share go out from the plains beyond the swampland. Lumber was also big, with logs being floated down the Saint Francis to several different lumber manufacturers that set up shop in the city, making everything from furniture to wagon parts to barrel staves.

The bustling city brought in immigrants who came up through New Orleans, looking for a jumping-off point to start their new lives in the New World. Sicilian, Italian, Bulgarian, Greek, Lebanese, Syrian and Chinese folk settled in Helena, joining established residents. Germans passed through on their way to settlements at Stuttgart and Ulm, and Swiss travelers went on to Barton and Hicks. Jews journeyed onward from the port to Jonesboro, Blytheville, Pine Bluff and Wynne. Mexican nationals came north to work the fields after the Civil War, while black Americans were able to find footholds in city government and leadership. The Helena of 1900 was a vibrant, multi-national melting pot of cultures.

Restaurants and groceries flourished for decades, including legendary spots such as Alvin Solomon's Helena Wholesale Dry Goods, Paul and George Garofas's Busy Bee Café, Tom Nick's People's Café, the Garofas family's Bell Café and Etoch Habib's eponymous café, which became famous for shipping fruitcakes nationwide.

In the early part of the twentieth century, developers began building northwest of town. In 1907, this new area was connected by a trolley system to the port. In 1917, the new city of West Helena was incorporated.

Sadly for both towns, the lumber manufacturing base was smacked with two problems—the development and expansion of automobiles (which eliminated the need for new wooden wagon parts) and Prohibition, which meant an end to the need for beer, whiskey and wine barrel staves. Both towns began a slow decline that would continue throughout the century.

On January 1, 2006, the cities merged into one, and Helena–West Helena was born. You can still tour downtown Helena, starting at the Delta Cultural Center (where the King Biscuit Hour, hosted every weekday by the legendary "Sunshine" Sonny Payne since 1951, is held) and passing by the buildings along Cherry Street that once housed many of those old restaurants. Sadly, few classic eateries remain in business. Still, one dining experience endures, thanks to the third generation of a Sicilian family that's responsible for the development of a Delta staple: the Arkansas Delta tamale.

PASQUALE'S TAMALES, HELENA–WEST HELENA

Every Friday and Saturday morning, a white trailer appears alongside U.S. Highway 49 in Helena–West Helena bearing a simple banner: TAMALES.

Throughout the day, cars pull up. Scents waft on the breeze, full of corn, beef and spices. While the trailer is new, the scent is ancient to the settled Delta. If you were to go to the window of the trailer, you would be greeted by Joe and Joyce St. Columbia.

The tamales are Joe's grandfather's recipe, but Joyce is the reason they're still being sold today. The tamales and the way they are made are a particular Arkansas Delta tradition, something that dates back more than a century.

Joe St. Columbia's grandfather Peter came to America in 1892, leaving behind his wife and only son in Cefalu, Sicily, to find his fortune. He landed in New Orleans all but penniless and got a job cutting sugar cane for fifty cents a day. He kept up that hard work until he had enough to buy passage up the Mississippi River.

He made it as far as Helena. Joe says it's possible his grandfather ran out of money. He was just the second Italian to make it to Helena, a town already full of Greeks, Germans, Lebanese, Chinese and Jews also seeking a better life in America. Peter looked for things he could do to make money. He was a smart man who could find his way, and by 1897, he'd made enough marketing wares and doing odd jobs to bring over his wife and son for a visit. They came through Ellis Island and then from New York by train—$300 for the entire journey. When they arrived and saw how well Peter was doing, they decided to stay.

He was able to pick up languages easily, and his Sicilian dialect of Italian wasn't so different from the Spanish spoken by the Mexican families who sent men to the fields to work cotton. He got to know many of them well, and they shared gossip and recipes. He taught them pasta making and Italian dishes, and they taught him how to make tamales. The tamales they made would include anything from chicken to pork to goat. They were the perfect portable meal to carry in the field, and they kept warm in a pocket. Since they were already packaged in corn husks, they had their own biodegradable container.

The recipe Peter put together for the Arkansas Delta tamale was a little different from what he was taught. Instead of the other meats, he used only beef, good cuts that were lower in fat, a finer ground mesa and plenty of spices. These he'd take out to the fields and sell to other farm workers.

The St. Columbia family prospered in the New World. Peter peddled wares, drove a taxi, ran a grocery store and made some investments. By the First World War, they were doing well, and he and his son, Sam, built and bought properties in downtown Helena. The Depression came about, and they still did just fine since Sam and Peter had never trusted the banks. While those around them lost their shirts, Peter managed to keep ahold of their properties and businesses and purchase more. As Joe related to me, it wasn't uncommon to hear people speak of the St. Columbia family as such: "Don't those damn [Italians] know how tough finances are, spending all that money?"

Sam's thought on the matter was: "If I do well during the Depression, when there's no more Depression, I'll be rich."

Around this time a couple, Eugene and Maggie Brown, approached him about renting out one of his buildings. They wanted to open a restaurant that sold soul food, sandwiches and pie. Sam saw he had a building that would just sit empty otherwise, and renting to these folks seemed a good investment. So he agreed to let them use the property on one condition—they had to use his recipe to make tamales. They did—altering it just a little bit.

The combination of a Mexican dish, recreated by an Italian and produced by an African American family as soul food created the Arkansas version of the Delta tamale. The Elm Street Tamale Shop took off, and it became quite well known, with folks coming out of the woodwork to get theirs. The couple did well, selling the tamales alongside other soul food like turnip greens, pig ears and sandwiches. They also built a pushcart and took it around from one juke joint to another on Walnut Street, with the chant, "One for a nickel, three for a dime. Sell a lot more, but there just ain't time."

The folks that ran the Elm Street Tamale Shop did well, and their kids grew up and headed to Detroit for jobs. The shop stayed open through World War II. Eventually, the couple died of old age, and Joe's two brothers bought it. They ran an Italian deli in the same spot for ten years, while still serving those tamales.

Joe, on the other hand, went into the insurance business and then into the ownership of a beer business he ran for some twenty-odd years. When his brothers folded up, that was it for tamales for a while. But there was a day when Mammie Davis (Joe's maid) and Joyce, Joe's wife, got a hankering for tamales. They got out the old recipe and started working those tamales and made a mess of them. Joe got home and had some, and they were good. Joyce said there was a real need for these tamales and they should start making them again. So they did, in the kitchen at the beer factory. Long story short, Joe restarted the business, except this time, it was all about making the tamales. His daughter-in-law, Rhonda, had done research and had found that Joe's dad, Sam, had the original first name Pasquale, which Sam hadn't cared to share because it sounded so foreign. Thus was born Pasquale's Tamales.

Joe got a factory going. The operation started off first as a hand-crank deal, with a lot of labor involved. Then the St. Columbias purchased a mechanical extruder and conveyor belt system, and they started making tamales in batches of 2,400.

They started a restaurant that sold Italian dishes alongside the tamales. They worked like mad, putting in eighteen-hour days. Tamales got hot in the region again, and they just kept going and going, until Joyce had a heart attack. Joe came to the realization that, although the tamale factory and the restaurant were going strong, both took a lot of their time and effort. And as Joe puts it, "all the money in Phillips County wouldn't be worth it without her."

The dust settled. Joe sold the tamale factory to a guy who—well, he had a heart attack, and Joe bought it back. He pared the operation back a lot. He stopped doing mail-order sales of tamales, got the cart and just did tamales two days a week, on Fridays and Saturdays.

And that's where you'll find them today, alongside U.S. Highway 49, usually selling every tamale they have before the day is done.

It's no wonder. There are no preservatives in these golden tubules of gastronomy—er, these tamales. They're made from finely ground cornmeal, chopped sirloin, fresh garlic and onion and a plethora of spices, steamed in corn husks and served hot. Everything's all-natural—no fillers, no lard, no bull. Well, of course, there's the sirloin.

It used to be that every single tamale was hand-wrapped in a corn shuck and tied with a bit more corn shuck that had been tied together, which was very time-consuming. One day, Joe came up with the idea of using a kitchen-friendly product similar to an elastic band like you use to pull back your hair. It's usually used to truss chicken legs, but Joe found it worked just as well for tying tamales. The corn shucks? Still tucked tight. Now the tamales are extruded, shuck-wrapped and tie-banded. They're cooked up together in what becomes the most amazing juice imaginable, a soup of spices and the flavors of corn, cornmeal and beef all together. When you order a sack, you get a cup of the juice to take with you. Just pull the tamales out of the box, put them in a dish and soak them in the juice. They're just as good as when you pick them up from the stand.

They are so good, in fact, that longtime Arkansas TV personality Chuck Dovish, back when he was the *Travelin' Arkansas* guy for Channel 11, told the audience that the tamales were "shuck-suckin' good." "You have to be real careful saying something like that," Joe told me. From that segment, the tagline of "suck the shuck" was born, and folks around here know you're talking about Pasquale's Tamales when you say those words.

BURGER SHACK, HELENA–WEST HELENA

Of the many restaurants that dot both sides of Helena–West Helena, few local eateries have survived the twenty-year mark. Of them, only one makes any major claim to a flavor tradition.

That place is the Burger Shack, a tiny little drive-in serving umpteen flavors of soft-serve, a smattering of burger-and-fry combinations and, as the signs on every side boast, the Best Coke in Town. Open since the 1960s, it's not unusual to find a line of cars snaked around the corner as patrons patiently wait their turn at the window.

> Helena is the birthplace of several famous musicians, including gospel maven Roberta Martin, blues legend Willie "Big Eyes" Smith, Grammy award–winning baritone William Warfield and the "High Priest of Country Music," Conway Twitty.

Yes, I have tried the Coke. Yes, I think it probably is the best in town. It has a sparkly, crisp, slightly citric bite that recalls the good days of Coca-Cola before all this "new" mush came about.

SHADDEN'S BAR-B-Q, MARVEL

They say a picture is worth a thousand words. In a single photograph of one little spot along U.S. Highway 49 in the little town of Marvell you'll find 100,000 sighs, the sighs of generations of hungry Arkansawyers, wishing again for a time that was and will probably never be again.

The photo would be that of a little paint-faded building beset with lean-tos, its screen doors shut for good and an aging wreath adorned with black ribbon tied to a handle. The wreath has been there since a couple days after the death of Wayne Shadden on May 21, 2010.

Shadden was the proprietor of a restaurant inside an old general store, a place that bore the name Shadden's Bar-B-Q. It has been oft reported that the place started out as a combination of barbecue joint and gambling hall, and that a $500 fine and a year in jail convinced Shadden to just concentrate on the 'cue.

The scent of pork butt smoke would pull you right off the road. If you hit it right and the gravel lot wasn't full of cars, you were in luck. You scooted past the guys sitting in chairs outside (if it wasn't hot as the devil and sometimes even if it was) and the big old freezer out front and through those screened doors. Inside you could get a burger, but you should have ordered the barbecue, sliced. The mild sauce was spicy, the hot nigh unbearable, and all of it meant to be consumed with an ice-cold beer. The sauce, by the way, was the contribution of Wayne's wife, Vivian, to the two-handed sandwiches.

As of this writing, it's been closed for four years, and since the Shadden kids all live out of state, chances are it's never coming back. But you can still enjoy the barbecue sauce. The recipe first appeared in the cookbook *High Cotton Cookin': A Collection of Southern Country Recipes*, published back in 1978 by the Marvell Academy Mothers' Association.

Shadden's BBQ Sauce

¼ cup oil
½ stick (4 tablespoons) butter
2 small onions, finely chopped
3 tablespoons Worcestershire sauce
½ bottle A-1 sauce
3 cups ketchup
1 tablespoon chili powder
2 tablespoons brown sugar
½ tablespoon Tabasco
¼ lemon (grated, including rind)
Salt and pepper to taste
Cayenne pepper to taste (for added heat)

Sauté the onions in butter and oil until tender. Add the other ingredients, mix well and cook for 30 to 45 minutes over medium heat.

Arkansas Highway 1, Marvel to Gillett

The great restaurants that hang on do so only because they've managed to make things work. But not all survive. Driving south from Marvell down Arkansas Highway 1 shows that. In DeWitt, Sahara's Family Restaurant has been up and running since 1981, but the fantastic melty cheeseburgers at Irene's are a thing of the past, and the old Don's Catfish is now used for karaoke (though Pat and Donald Vansandt's granddaughter, Lizzie Stubblefield, had a self-named place of her own on the downtown square for a while). You can still get a bite off the buffet at The Willows, or you could end up at Troy's Drive In.

Troy's is just another old-fashioned dairy diner. Its Facebook page simply calls it "an old joint with good food," and that's pretty much it—great fountain drinks, hamburgers and fries, soft-serve ice cream. Nothing decadent.

Keep heading down Arkansas Highway 1, which the Great River Road follows, and you'll eventually end up at a little town with a nationwide reputation. For one night in January each year, it's the center of the political universe.

The Gillett Coon Supper

Gillett is a town of just 691 people along Arkansas's Great River Road. It's a small community built around agriculture and southern tradition. But on one day each year, the town doubles in size in the first act of a year's political drama. Every Arkansas politician of any renown has come through Gillett at one time or another, including the most famous of our native-born sons.

This is not that story. As Alton Brown so succinctly put it, "I'm here for the food."

To talk about Gillett's Coon Supper is to reference not one event, but two. The larger event happens each year as it has every year since 1933 (except during World War II) in the old high school gymnasium. The smaller event began in the 1970s. There was a gentleman who lived across the street from that high school; he and his wife would open their home for a party each year before the get-together. That young man eventually decided to run for office, and the party became a political fundraiser. When Representative Marion Berry came home from Congress, the party became a different sort of fundraiser—one that sends two Gillett high school seniors to college each year. The party remains a part of Arkansas tradition, though now it's held on the Berry Farm rather than in the house in town.

We came into the Arkansas County town from Stuttgart via DeWitt with the singular direction, from my friend Gabe Holstrom, to "follow the Berry signs." Down a gravel road, still somewhat slick from rain, way out into the verdant and soggy plain of an Arkansas field planted in the past year with corn, a right turn past a rice paddy, a left turn onto a road headed out to a set of outbuildings. There were cars parked side by side near what appeared to be a hangar. Outside, three men tended a smoker while two young boys threw rocks into a puddle.

My daughter, Hunter, had come along for the ride, and she played shy with the kids while I made introductions and found my direction. The men were lording over long skewers of bacon-wrapped meat in the chilly air.

It was 3:30 p.m. on the dot. Concerned that we would be late to the party, we'd arrived on time, and within the hangar there was just a scattering of people tidying up the last minute details. These included making sure sponsor banners were in place, the bar was fully stocked and a long table was loaded with food. Each item appeared to have been brought by someone local. There were cubes of cheese; thin slices of salami and smoked ham; a duck prosciutto; homemade pancetta, naked-looking and soft; vegetable trays; fruit trays; a spread of crackers and a cheese ball; and that strange blob of cream cheese covered in sauce you see at any gathering these days. There was a large cooler of peeled and deveined shrimp with sauce, a pile of soft rolls and a roaster full of venison stew packed with onions, carrots and potatoes.

And then there were the meats—not the deli meats but the hearty, bone-sticking meat you'd expect to sustain one through winter. From the smoker came pork butts, which the ladies in the back would break open, shred and platter. There were big links of sausage too. And there were Duck Bites. The Arkansas Delta, after all, is known for its duck. Nearby Stuttgart is the Duck and Rice Capital of the World, and the season was still underway. These appetizers were the skewered bacon-wrapped parcels on the smoker I saw coming in, containing parmesan-breaded jalapeno-stuffed slices of wild duck that were only pulled when they started to char.

Gabe had told me these would go quick—and they did. Though there might have been fifty pounds pulled from the smoke, they went quickly into the mouths and onto the plates of the individuals who came to the line. When they were gone, they were replaced with fall-apart smoked turkey and chicken.

At 4:08 p.m. on the dot, the crowd swelled in, first individuals pulling up in their own vehicles, and then the crowd that came aboard the Little Rock Tours bus. The empty farm hangar went from hollow echoes to a solid block of sound in seconds. Through the door they came, man and woman, a collection of suits, padded vests and ties and young men bearing campaign stickers for every flavor of Arkansas politician. Amongst the politicians and business leaders, there were folks with camera and pad in hand, like me, jostling about. The journalists, the TV crews, the newspaper folks and the radio guys, we found ourselves suddenly surrounded by subjects. Interviews commenced left and right as fellows clapped one another on the back, and young ladies giggled. Cameras beeped as the crowd filed in and filled out. The room became so loud a coherent conversation between any but the most able lip-readers was conducted in a series of smiles and nods.

And then there was a break, as if the crowd had simultaneously reached the moment to take a breath or a swig of a beverage. At the door, there was a rustle and former congressman Marion Berry came in the room. A swarm of people formed the most disorganized circular line in an effort to get a chance to thank him for his hospitality.

The governor was there. ABC and MSNBC were there. A progressive-country band was playing in the corner, providing a soundtrack for the whole mess. Some 220 people turned out for the pre-supper party, and the resulting crowd brought around $20,000 into the scholarship fund. This particular gathering could be considered nothing but a success. But, as I said, I came for the food. Soon enough it was time to head for the other event.

We arrived at the former Gillett High School a few minutes before 6:00 p.m. There weren't a lot of people in town at that point, and we were able to park in the lot. I hustled quickly over to the gym door with Hunter, jogging a bit to get there as I saw the glint of metal. I had expected to see cooking on the premises, but I realized at that moment that the cooking was already done.

What I was seeing was a line of men, young and old, wearing white aprons. They were darting back and forth from a truck into the building with aluminum trays of food. They were swift and organized, passing through the double doors into the gymnasium's hall in shifts. I snapped a few shots and tried to keep out of the way.

Inside, two ladies sat at a table offering caps, ties and T-shirts by the main door to the interior. Across from them, a uniformed man stood at the ticket counter. This was for people to claim their tickets—the dinner had been sold out for weeks.

Within, the finely orchestrated work had begun. The tables were already set with commemorative glasses, Styrofoam plates and numbered programs, eight hundred in all. On both sides of the gym, there were tables in the low concrete bleachers along each side. A musician was warming up on the stage, and there were places set right next to it as well. Every inch of space was taken.

The men worked in teams. Shifts of aluminum tray–carrying guys went to tables, where they set deep tins of coon, ribs and brisket. Others functioned in sets—one man holding a tray of sweet potatoes while another dolloped out a serving on each plate. The same went for the cakes, rolls and rice. They were working as fast as they could—the doors would open promptly at 6:30 p.m.

Each setting was identical: a plate filled with sides, a glass with a cup inside and tins of meat. What was different was what sat next to the rolls: a slice of cake, each different but all individually wrapped in plastic—golden vanilla, chocolate Bundt, chocolate-iced (not frosted) vanilla, peanut butter, chocolate-iced chocolate, strawberry, spice, carrot, cream cheese–topped butter cake. There were so many varieties. The cakes were all made by ladies in town, who sliced and wrapped those pieces before handing them over to the Farmers and Businessmen Club, which oversees putting the Coon Supper together. Everything at the Gillett Coon Supper is donated or sponsored.

Then there's the coon. Do people really eat raccoon at the Coon Supper? Why, yes they do. Originally, just raccoon was served—two thousand pounds of it for up to twelve hundred people. Over the years, that has changed. No longer is the eating of the coon something that political candidates needed to gobble like a freshman's fraternity hazing. No, today baby-back pork ribs and beef brisket are also offered—thanks to Jennings Osborne. The beloved Arkansas philanthropist sponsored the dinner for many years, bringing in his epic grills and smokers and serving up barbecued meats alongside the coon. Osborne passed away a few years ago, and the Farmers and Businessman Group managed to find other sponsors.

The coon is harvested by people in the community who set traps for the furry mammals. For a couple months before the event, a stand alongside Arkansas Highway 1 offers $1.68 a pound for each one brought in. A normal-sized raccoon will garner three to four pounds of meat. In 2014, seven hundred pounds worth of raccoon was trapped, purchased and smoked.

By this point in the evening, a line started to form outside, and the other journalists were arriving to find their spots. Many sought politicians such as Senator Mark Pryor, Attorney General Dustin McDaniel, former

Tables line the halls from one end to another with just enough room to pass by inside the Gillett High School gymnasium for the annual Gillett Coon Supper. *Grav Weldon.*

congressmen Asa Hutchinson and Mike Ross and current (as of this writing) Representative Tom Cotton. But Arkansas politicians weren't the only lawmakers on the guest book. Senators Dick Durbin of Illinois, Angus King of Maine and Joe Donelly of Indiana were in attendance—all three guests of Senator Pryor. The Gillett Coon Supper might as well be a mandatory campaign obligation for any lawmaker planning to make it in Arkansas. Governor Beebe says this Coon Supper was his thirty-second.

The mayor himself welcomed people into the gym and pointed them toward their seats. Each row of tables sat fifty to a side, and helpful volunteers ushered folks into place.

So what did the coon taste like? I'll let Grav tell you: "It starts out nice and smokey, but there's too much smoke, and then it's just something I'm not sure I should have in my mouth."

Hunter, at the brilliant age of five, described it thusly: "It tastes like ash. I mean, like it's already burnt."

Raccoon, in my opinion, is best served stewed or soaked well in broth with dumplings. It's wild meat of course, gray and a bit stringy. To say it's an acquired taste overstates the obvious.

I happened to catch sight of the governor as he came in laughing. He was telling a reporter from one of the newspapers that this was likely his last Coon Supper, since his days in office were nearly over. Governor Beebe gets this crowd, though, and he did his own measure of chuckling as he shook hands and posed for photographs. His tenure here may be long, but it's not unprecedented. I met one gentleman who's been coming for fifty-six years, and a lady who had attended or cooked at the supper for more than sixty. I also met beauty queens who squeamishly nibbled at their perfunctory piece of coon meat, grimacing for the cameras; young boys who relished the adventure of eating as many animals as possible in one sitting; and young men attending with their camouflaged-and-booted girlfriends. There was far more talking than eating, for sure. But there was indeed eating taking place while hands met and flesh pressed, a night of eating, listening and a whole lot of talking.

There's no alcohol served at the Gillett Coon Supper (unlike the Berry Farm party) for a multitude of reasons, which I'm sure have a lot to do not just with community preferences, but also the lack of places to put up those that might need to sleep it off (the Rice Paddy Motel has just fourteen rooms). But there's really no need to lubricate tongues in a crowd like this.

We left before the crowd could exit en masse. For six blocks around the school there were cars lined up on both sides of the road, with barely a car's width in between to squeeze through. Past the parking, the town was quiet and empty, block after block of silent homes lit by streetlamps and the ancient Christmas decorations still lining the roads.

Gillett is a town of just 691 people. Its school only offers classes from kindergarten through the fifth grade. Older kids go to DeWitt schools twelve miles away. It's as flat as a pancake, and its downtown is a collection of lonely buildings without tenants, save the local bank. But the sign on Arkansas Highway 1 says it all: Welcome to Gillett, Home of Friendly People and the Coon Supper. And for one day each year, it's the center of Arkansas.

Gabe Holstrom's Duck Bites

4 duck breasts
4 ounces Dale's Steak Seasoning Sauce (available at dalesseasoning.com)
1 cup breadcrumbs
1 cup Parmesan cheese
1 12-ounce package sliced bacon
1–2 cups sliced jalapeños (number needed will vary based on size of breast)
Pepperjack cheese (optional), to taste
Toothpicks
1 batch Duck Bite Remoulade (see recipe)

Slice duck breasts into bite-sized pieces, roughly 1 inch wide by 1–2 inches long. Marinate in Dale's Seasoning Sauce for 30 minutes. In bowl, combine breadcrumbs and Parmesan cheese. Roll each piece of duck in the mixture. Slice the bacon into 3 inch pieces. Drain the jalapeños. To assemble: wrap each piece of duck around a piece of jalapeño (and pepperjack cheese, if using), then wrap in bacon and secure with a toothpick. Cook in a preheated oven at 350 degrees or on grill at medium heat until internal temperature of the duck reaches 155 degrees. Remove from heat; the meat will continue to heat up for a few minutes. Serve with special remoulade.

Duck Bite Remoulade

1 cup mayo
1–2 tablespoons ketchup (more ketchup makes a sweeter sauce)
2–3 tablespoons Creole or large grain mustard
1 teaspoon Worchestershire sauce
1 teaspoon Tabasco sauce
2–3 green onions, finely chopped
Juice of ½ lemon, squeezed
Salt and pepper to taste

Combine all ingredients and chill 30 minutes before serving.

THE RICE PADDY MOTEL AND RESTAURANT, GILLETT

I mentioned the Rice Paddy Motel and Restaurant. Locals just call the eatery the Motel. Inside you'll find good country cooking, a seafood buffet on Friday nights and good Delta catfish any day of the week.

I talked with town historian John Cover about the place. Though he was just a child when the motel and restaurant opened in 1957, he can tell you a bunch of things about it. For one, the motel used to just have four or five rooms and the restaurant was far more diner than country buffet. You could go in and sit on a stool at the counter and have yourself a cold drink or a sandwich, back in the day.

The Rice Paddy was built and started by Johnny and Herbert Holzhauer and their father, John. "Papa John" might have been the one to name the place.

"Papa" John Holzhauer once planted a small paddy of rice in front of the Rice Paddy and Motel in Gillett. *Grav Weldon.*

"I do remember," Cover told me, "right out in front, around the main sign, still the basis of the sign today, Papa John plowed up a little place about twenty feet wide and forty feet long and grew him rice there every year. And Papa John took care of the rice. Of course, every field around it had rice in it too—we're out here in the middle of rice country. We had a little rice paddy for the restaurant and motel."

The motel and restaurant survived, thanks to traffic along U.S. Highway 165 after it was paved and to the workers from river projects over several years. From 1963 to 1969, there were skilled men employed in the big McClellan-Kerr Arkansas River Navigation System project; in the 1990s through 2002, construction was completed on the nearby Montgomery Point Lock and Dam at the mouth of the White River. Today, during the hunting season, hunters coming through the area keep the Paddy hopping. But any time of year, you'll find it filled with locals seeking a plate of catfish or a burger.

ARKANSAS POST

The Great River Road follows Arkansas Highway 1 down from Gillett on south. It passes Arkansas Post, originally a trading post established in 1686 by Henri de Tonti, an Italian-born French explorer. It's also the site of the very last battle of the American Revolution. By the end of the eighteenth century, the post, formerly favored by French fur traders, had become a Spanish holding. The Spanish were allies of the Revolutionary forces. On April 17, 1783, a force of roughly one hundred British-allied white and Native American volunteers attacked the Spanish garrison of Fort Carlos III at Arkansas Post. Remembered as "Colbert's Raid," the battle ended in a Spanish victory, thanks to a bold defense waged by the soldiers holding the fort.

The post became part of the Louisiana Purchase in 1803, and in 1819 Arkansas Post was selected as the first territorial capital of Arkansas. The state's first newspaper, the *Arkansas Gazette*, was printed there in 1819 (today the *Arkansas Democrat-Gazette* is considered the oldest newspaper west of the Mississippi River).

Fort Hindman, a Confederate fort, was built on the peninsula out into the Arkansas River early on in the Civil War. It was overcome by Union forces during a two-day barrage on January 10 and 11, 1863.

Unlike the Blue Ridge Parkway, the Natchez Trace Parkway and other nationally designated roads of this nature, the Great River Road is not monitored by the National Parks Service. Instead, it's a collection of existing roads mostly updated to parkway conditions. Originally conjured in 1938 and designated a national scenic byway in 2005, the series of roads from the Canadian border to the Gulf of Mexico offer leisure travelers a chance to see sights of historical, cultural and geographical interest along its length.

Most of the Great River Road in Arkansas lies along established two-lane and four-lane highways. However, there are stretches that utilize neighborhood streets. A small section that runs concurrent with County Road 239 north of Helena along Crowley's Ridge remains unpaved. For more information about the Great River Road, check out Arkansas.com/GRR. For a map of the entire route, go to ExperienceMississippiRiver.com.

Today, two parks mark what's left of Arkansas Post—a national site commemorating the American Revolution, the Civil War and Arkansas's first capital and a state park that preserves the history of life in the Delta and the Grand Prairie. For more information, check out nps.gov/arpo.

Arkansas Highway 1 South to Watson

Arkansas Highway 1 crosses the Arkansas River at Pendleton, where a tiny mobile home community has sprung up under the bridge. This was once the home of Pendleton Sandbar, a friendly little restaurant serving fishermen and river rats looking for a bite.

Just south of Back Gate, Arkansas Highway 1 diverges southeast from U.S. Highway 165, which continues on to Dumas. Two lanes of blacktop pass by fields of cotton and soybeans, rustic farms and rural houses, down to the community of Watson.

Once a thriving small town, there's not much in Watson any more. Even the railroad tracks are gone, replaced by a growing asphalt path that will one day link Lexa and Helena–West Helena to the north with Dumas to the south. The Union Pacific Railroad donated for park use what will become Delta Heritage Trail State Park once it's complete, covering nearly eighty-five miles, making it the longest state park in Arkansas.

If you were to follow that trail northeastward, you'd eventually come to the Arkansas River and the Yancopin Bridge—a nearly mile-long abandoned railbridge. An old lift span on one end now sits permanently anchored in the down position, since the river's shift over the years have left nothing but sand under it. One of the middle sections is a swing span that is opened to allow taller boats and logging barges through. It's situated twenty miles upriver from the Mississippi, at the location of a former community called Yancopin that replaced the town of Napoleon when it was swallowed by both rivers. Yancopin was never incorporated. It got its name from either the corruption of an old Indian word (chinquapin) or from the old Yankee holding area there, the "yankee pen."

Bonnie's Café, Watson

Watson is home to a post office, a liquor store and a single restaurant with a blue-painted aluminum façade and a Coca-Cola sign marking Bonnie's Café.

Watson isn't really near anything, unless you count the Rohwer War Relocation Center National Historic Site a few miles to the south. For Watson, though, Bonnie's is the heart of the community. Since 1985, owner Bonnie Davidson has been serving breakfast and lunch six days a week to the folks who come through the door.

Bonnie Davidson's place is decorated with old saws, maps and other items from around the town of Watson. *Grav Weldon.*

We dropped in one Thursday morning, were greeted kindly in the almost empty restaurant and were told we could have breakfast or lunch. There was no menu, just an ancient, age-yellowed board on the wall. Our hostess brought us massive Mason jars of beverages and took our orders, and we quietly waited while she went to the back and got things started.

The day's average patrons dribbled through. It was too early for a full lunch but not too early for pickups. A guy the hostess called Lee came in. Before he was halfway to the register in the back, she started to holler: "Mayo and ketchup, right?" He nodded, and she continued, "Fries ain't done yet, it'll be a few." Lee gave her a nod and a gesture and went out front to sit on one of the two van benches located to either side of the front door.

"So how long have you been here?" I asked across the room.

"About twenty-five years now," she hollered back, continuing to work on our meals.

A younger lady, perhaps in her forties, came through the doors and entered the middle of a conversation. I caught "she done died up in the hills. She was ninety-six years old, never did have no kids."

I looked back out front where Lee was waiting. I saw him get up and turn to come inside. The hostess met him halfway across the room with a couple white sacks. He nodded and turned out. I have no idea if any money was exchanged.

The Rohwer War Relocation Center was a World War II Japanese-American internment camp located in rural southeastern Arkansas, in Desha County. The camp housed, along with the Jerome camp, some sixteen thousand Japanese Americans from September 18, 1942, to November 30, 1945, and was one of the last of ten such camps to close. The Japanese American population had been forcibly removed from the West Coast of America under the doctrine of "military necessity" and incarcerated in ten relocation camps in California and various states west of the Mississippi River. Its internees include *Star Trek* actor and LGBT activist George Takei. The World War II Japanese-American Internment Museum, located in nearby McGehee, commemorates the camp's existence and the individuals held there.

I'd no more than jotted down a few notes about the exchange when our lunches arrived. Grav's lunch special was a smothered country-fried steak, potatoes and great northern beans, the former two doused in a somewhat-thin brown gravy, all of it steamy and smelling like a country kitchen. The beefsteak was crunchy and fork-tender, lovingly and lightly spiced with salt and pepper and maybe a little seasoning salt. It was a generous hand-sized portion, about one-half-inch thick. The potatoes were hand-mashed; the beans were slow-cooked and buttery, and I snuck some off his plate. Our hostess noticed when she came to deliver a hunk of cornbread and a biscuit, and she brought me back a bean bowl of my own.

Not that I needed more food. The one-third pound flat-smashed patty on my burger was crusty from the griddle and glued to the top bun by a single slice of American cheese, like what you'd get at a drive-in restaurant. Still, I ended up sneaking Grav's cornbread off his plate to pinch into my beans. It was soft and yellow, slightly sweet and buttery.

Our hostess came out and asked about dessert. Both of us refused at first, but she told us she'd bring us a small piece. She returned with a corner slice of buttermilk cake, a basic butter cake, similar to a pound cake, with a little cinnamon and that tang you only get with buttermilk. I ended up eating every bit.

The Great River Road splits at Back Gate, with the westward branch sliding over to Dumas via U.S. Highway 165 and the eastern branch following Arkansas Highway 1. They meet again in McGehee on U.S. Highway 65. South of town, rolling fields are criss-crossed with bayous, all the way down to Lake Village.

2
LAKE VILLAGE

Lake Village has served as the seat of Chicot County since 1857. It sits on Lake Chicot, the largest oxbow lake in North America. If you've read *Classic Eateries of the Ozarks and Arkansas River Valley*, you may already know its claim to fame. It goes back to Italy, to New York banker Austin Corbin's purchase of the Sunnyside Plantation and his arrangement for immigrants from Rome to populate the settlement. It ends hundreds of miles away in northwest Arkansas, with the establishment of Tontitown. The middle of the story lies in this agrarian community.

After Father Pietro Bandini and the thiry-five families who followed him to northwest Arkansas established Tontitown, Bandini sent word to Italy for another minister for the people of Sunnyside. That fell to Father F.J. Galloni, who arrived on the plantation a short time later and who would eventually move to Lake Village proper.

Italians were also recruited to other plantations in the area. When Lake Village was officially incorporated in 1898 (the same year as Tontitown), its makeup included many of those Italian settlers as well as whites and blacks whose families had lived there long before.

Italian heritage is still celebrated in Lake Village each March with the annual spaghetti dinner at Our Lady of the Lake Church. The celebration takes weeks of preparation, with bread baked and egg-yolk noodles made in January and the Pierini family rolling 3,600 meatballs every February. The whole community contributes to the making of desserts.

A FRIED CHICKEN HISTORY

The immigrants who followed Father Bandini to Tontitown took with them not only their own spaghetti but also fried chicken, the latter being a part of Delta custom long before their arrival. Born of similar dishes brought across the South by both African and Scottish ancestors, the traditional fried chicken served as "Sunday's best" is still prevalent today.

Mind you, the original meat of Arkansas was pork, because pigs can be raised anywhere, on anything. Yardbird was a special-occasion food, something you ended up bringing to the church social. Fried chicken was considered "Yankee Dinner"—a term used first by nineteenth-century newspaperman William Minor "Cush" Quesenbury, who called visiting northerners "chicken-eaters."

Most settlers from Europe were accustomed to having their chicken roasted or stewed. The Scots are believed to have brought the idea of frying chicken in fat to the United States and eventually into the Arkansas Delta in the eighteenth and nineteenth centuries. Similarly, African slaves brought to the South were sometimes allowed to keep chickens, which didn't take up much space. They flour-breaded their pieces of plucked poultry, popped it with paprika and saturated it with spices before putting it into the grease. Frying in lard or oil is quicker than baking and could be done in a cast-iron vessel over a fire or on a stove. It didn't take long for that propensity for jointing and processing chicken with the skin on; dipping it in flour, buttermilk and egg; and dropping into a hot skillet to take hold.

Chicken was battered and fried in southeast Arkansas for decades before the arrival of those Italian immigrants who bought into Sunnyside Plantation. But they picked it up quickly once they arrived. Those who didn't move on to Tontitown would remain in Sunnyside for the duration, and just like with Peter St. Columbia up in Helena, they shared their Italian gastronomic identity by adapting the dish.

Today, you can still find pretty dang good fried chicken around the area. JJ's Café (which was JJ's Lakeside Café until it moved into town) still offers an excellent version on its lunch buffet. There are fast-food versions, too. And then there's the fried chicken at a restaurant known not for that dish, but for tamales.

Rhoda's Famous Hot Tamales, Lake Village

There's been many a time I ended up on the doorstep of Rhoda Adams, the proprietress of a local establishment in Lake Village known as Rhoda's Famous Hot Tamales. She and her husband, James, run this place on Saint Mary's Street, and you can smell it a block away, the scent of spices and fried things luring you off the highway.

> In April 1923, Lake Village became the site of famed aviator Charles Lindbergh's first nighttime flight.

On one trip in March 2011, Grav and I picked up a dozen tamales in a paper sack from Rhoda on the way to New Orleans. We got on down the road, going through Eudora to hit Interstate 20 in Tallulah, Louisiana. Not far from Mound, traffic came to a dead stop. We waited on the pavement a while, and when traffic scooted up to a state trooper standing by the road, we asked him what was going on. Turns out a barge had hit the Mississippi Bridge at Vicksburg, and an inspector was on the way to make sure it was safe.

Rhoda Adams has been making tamales and pies at her establishment in Lake Village since 1973. *Courtesy JJ's Café.*

We did what most anyone would do—pulled off the road and waited in the one spot where there was space—the parking lot of an adult store. Being hungry, we dug into that sack of tamales.

We tore open that bag to find an aluminum foil–wrapped bundle. Through that, there was newspaper—a lot of it. I unwound the newspaper to find another aluminum foil–wrapped bundle, and through that there was wax paper and more aluminum foil and a paper boat that had all but disintegrated from the juice of a dozen cornhusk-wrapped beef-and-chicken-fat tamales. With no utensils in the car, we ate the tamales with our fingers. At that moment, it was the best thing I'd ever eaten in my life.

Rhoda knows her tamales are good. She never made a tamale in her life until someone said she should. That night, her family sat up together making tamales, wrapping them in cornhusks and tieing them until the wee hours. The next day she sold every single one. She still usually sells them all, but that's partly because she's such a good saleswoman. Every day except Sunday, Rhoda gets up and packs hot tamales a dozen in a bag, three dozen in a coffee can, as many as she thinks she can part with, and puts them in her van. She then drives around town selling them. She goes to the RV parks, to the banks of Lake Chicot and to the parking lot of home furnishings legend Paul Michael's (where staffers will tell you how she honks, sometimes until customers vacate the store) and sells them. Then she heads back to her restaurant for the lunch rush.

Rhoda started with sweet potato pie (*Arkansas Pie: A Delicious Slice of the Natural State* will tell you more about that). She's famous for her tamales, not just because they're good but because she does good press. She can also talk the legs off a mule; I was in town with a group of my colleagues a few years ago, determined not to take home more than one of those little three-inch pies for lunch. I walked in, got my lunch and she told me I was going to buy one of her half-and-half pecan and sweet potato pies. And she was right, I did.

But Rhoda's also a master of another Arkansas staple: fried chicken. It's an exquisite, salty, juicy, orange-gold bird meant for consumption with white bread and sweet potatoes, preferably with sweet tea.

She started the operation in 1973, and a fair number of folks have come through in all those years—from television producers and politicians to regular folks like you and me. And she's still convincing folks to walk out of her establishment full, happy and with a pie to go.

You can see Rhoda's husk-wrapped tamales on the back cover of this book.

KOWLOON RESTAURANT, LAKE VILLAGE

In several cities across the Arkansas Delta, you'll find Chinese restaurants that have been open for decades, run by the descendants of immigrants who came looking for the fabled Gaam San, or Golden Mountain. They settled along the Mississippi River Delta and Crowley's Ridge. Some stuck with agricultural work but many opened small grocery stores, and after the stores came the restaurants. Cantonese flavors are still popular with diners throughout the Arkansas Delta.

In Lake Village, there remains Kowloon Restaurant. Back in the 1970s, the Lee family operated a small grocery store in town. But Arthur "Pat" Lee realized that when other larger grocery stores such as Yee's Food Giant moved in he wouldn't be able to keep up. He'd had a hand in a restaurant in Little Rock, the Hong Kong Restaurant on Cantrell Road, and he decided to give it a shot in Lake Village. Kowloon opened February 24, 1977, and is still going strong.

Locals came in and liked what they ate, and news spread. Today, the Mongolian beef, sweet-and-sour chicken and all the favorites of traditional Chinese restaurants are offered here. Pat's son, Arthur Lee Jr., still runs the place and says all that's really changed is that the menu has been simplified a little over the years.

The name of the restaurant? The senior Lee hailed from Hong Kong, which is where the Little Rock's restaurant got its name. Kowloon is named for Mrs. Lee's hometown.

Kowloon Restaurant in Lake Village. *Grav Weldon*.

The Cow Pen, Lake Village

Lake Chicot, on which Lake Village sits, is the largest oxbow lake in North America and the largest natural lake in Arkansas. It formed when the Mississippi River changed its channel, leaving behind a crescent-shaped body of water known for its crappie, largemouth bass and channel catfish. It gets its name from the French word for "stumpy," thanks to all the cypress trees and knees along the lake's banks.

Lake Village is where U.S. Highways 65 and 82 pair up before they dance across the Mississippi on what is now the longest cable-stayed bridge across Big Muddy at Greenville. At the foot of the new Greenville Bridge lies an old cattle inspection station that's been renovated, burned out and renovated again. This is the Cow Pen, purveyor of some of the best steaks you'll find in the Delta, and home of the Chip and Dip.

Floyd Owens bought the old station back in 1967 and turned it into something new. He started a restaurant to serve the folks coming across the old Benjamin G. Humphreys Bridge from Greenville. Ten years later, he turned it over to Gene and Juanita Grassi, who ran it for thirty years. They added other items, ranging from catfish to Mexican fare to the Italian dishes popular in the area.

The Grassis decided to retire in 2007 and handed the reins over to Charles Faulk and his family. Sadly, six months later the place burned out. That didn't deter the Faulks, who dove into the task of rebuilding it bigger and better. Since reopening in November 2008, the place has flourished.

You can't really get a seat in the place Friday and Saturday nights, not right away at least. Within the wood-clad walls of the place, folks pack every section. I've seen parties there of grown men with the charisma of little boys, telling stories and bragging over their steaks. I've seen elegantly dressed individuals pile in after weddings and gamblers who've crossed the bridge looking for something not served in a casino.

There was even a time when I came looking for sustenance and found it in the form of Chip and Dip—a palatial basket of fresh-fried, thin tortilla chips served with six-ounce metal ramekins of housemade bean dip, housemade salsa and bright yellow cheese dip.

The Cow Pen Restaurant in Lake Village. *Grav Weldon.*

Any Tuesday through Saturday night (or any Sunday lunch), you might see Big Charles, Teresa, Little Charles, Lydia, Ed, Cookie, Angela, Jose, Bill or Sue Anne. Everyone's on a first-name basis, and you might as well be home.

BELOW LAKE VILLAGE

Lake Village lies at a crossroads. In 1918, the first section of Arkansas Highway A-3 was completed through town; this became part of U.S. Highway 65 when it was created in 1926. Arkansas Highway 2 once crossed the city, tied to Greenville on one side and all the way to Texarkana on the other. It became U.S. Highway 82 in 1932.

Not far from the city's western border you'll find Bayou Bartholomew, the longest bayou in the world. This 364-mile-long body of water separates the Delta's long, unbroken plain with the densely wooded Timberlands of this state—the border of the area covered by this book.

There aren't many restaurants in Chicot County outside of Lake Village—a handful in Eudora (none very old) and a few in Dermott (including

Willy's Old Fashioned Hamburgers, once a popular burger stop). Way down U.S. Highway 165 there's a little town called Wilmot that hugs the bayou where you'll find Country Cupboard, open for decades in a little dilapidated building across the street from the railroad tracks.

Most eateries lie along or not far from U.S. Highway 65 on the western side of the Lower Delta. Let's head that way.

3

U.S. HIGHWAY 65

McGehee

Up the road in McGehee, there are a few places worth stopping in. One of those is Kelley Drug and Selections, a local pharmacy that's also home to a gift shop, sandwich shop and soda fountain. That soda fountain and backbar date back to another facility. The owners of Kelley Drug rescued it from another business demolition and had it restored.

The hardwood fountain backbar at Kelley Drug and Selections dates back a century. *Grav Weldon*.

Though not technically "classic," Hoots BBQ deserves mention. David and Suzie Powell spent a couple years after retirement traveling from place to place by RV. When they grew tired of that, they decided to head back to their hometown of McGehee and open up a barbecue joint. The restaurant gets its name from the high school mascot, the McGehee Owl. Their eclectic tastes and nostalgic collection of restaurant items have been put to good use in decorating Hoot's BBQ, with recycled and reclaimed décor from dozens of different locations. The barbecue is also divine. They serve great pulled pork, chopped beef, burgers and some of the best onion rings in the region.

PICKENS COMMISSARY, NEAR DUMAS

The R.A. Pickens and Son Commissary started out in 1881 as the Pickens Plantation at Walnut Lake, south of Dumas. At one point, some five hundred people were employed in the various enterprises on the land, which included everything from cotton farming and ginning to a sawmill. Today, it's still a busy hub and home to a great southeast Arkansas restaurant and country store.

Folks around these parts call it the Commissary. Before 1948, farmers and their families would come to the commissary to purchase staples, trade and sell crops and gather to share news and enjoy a bite. There was always something to eat readily available at the counter, such as jerky or colas or fried pies.

The original structure, which bore the common general store look we're accustomed to, burned in 1948. The building that replaced it is a long brick structure with a curved roof reminiscent of a Quonset hut. Every Monday through Friday from seven to five o'clock, the store is open. Breakfast is good, but lunch is better. The baked chicken, covered in herbs and spices, is a particularly fantastic standout. Others are just as well loved, including the meatloaf and the fried salmon patty. Then there are all the side items—regional favorites like turnip greens, sweet potatoes, broccoli-and-cheese casserole, stewed squash, rice and gravy, deviled eggs, stewed cabbage and lima beans and best of all is the squash casserole. You order at the counter and then go claim a table and get your condiments. They'll call your name when your food is ready, you go get it and you eat it at a table in the middle of a room running all sorts of businesses around its edges—grocery store, apparel shop, post office and community center; at one time, there was even a bank. The conversations can get loud but never mean, and the clientele comes from every walk of life.

On any given day, there are coconut and chocolate meringue pies. Some days there will be peach pie, others strawberry (topped with whipped cream). Really, it's whatever is available at the time.

These days, the folks at Pickens keep a banner-clad trailer out by U.S. Highway 65 pointing the way to the community about a mile off the road. Most travelers whiz on by, never knowing what they're passing up. Now you know better.

Pic-Nic-Ker Drive In, Dumas

If you're a Dumas resident, you probably have had a burger at the Pic-Nic-Ker Drive In. The tiny, brown box on the corner of Waterman and Cherry Streets is the work of Mary Jenkins. She saw a need—a whole side of the town where there wasn't a place to eat—and started up the Pic-Nic-Ker Drive In on July 4, 1974. Forty years later, the little brown building where Arkansas Highway 54 makes a hard right is still hopping.

"I have some of my family that helps me out from time to time," Jenkins told me, "but I'm in here every day myself, doing my own cooking. It's a hobby of mine."

Every day, Jenkins comes in to cook, preparing Polish (fat sausages on buns), burgers and barbecue. In the summertime, kids ride their bikes over for ice cream.

When the restaurant opened, there were just two other fast food establishments in town (Big Banjo is one of them), and both were out by

The Pic-Nic-Ker in downtown McGehee. *Grav Weldon.*

For barbecue, you go to Hall's BBQ. Open since 1989, it's become a Main Street community standard—but if you haven't lived in town and you don't know someone from the area, you may have never have heard of it. *Grav Weldon*.

U.S. Highway 65. Today, most of the restaurants in town line that street, but the Pic-Nic-Ker keeps on going, the heart of a neighborhood that thrives on the little brown shop.

TAYLOR'S GROCERY/TAYLOR'S STEAKHOUSE, DUMAS

A lot of folks know about Taylor's Grocery in Mississippi—a rather famous grocery store that's now a marvelous catfish restaurant. Did you know there's a Taylor's just outside of Dumas? Both are locations where groceries were once sold that now house great restaurants.

Charles and Dorothy Taylor opened Taylor's Grocery in 1954. The original shotgun-style country house was pretty small, but it functioned like a traditional country store, a place to buy dry goods and foods and share a little gossip. In 1961, the Taylors moved the operation one-quarter mile closer to town into a larger building. They sold that store in the 1970s and opened up a third spot; in 1983, the fourth move happened, placing the business where it is now, far from the outskirts of Dumas.

Now, I mentioned grocery store. This book is all about restaurants (though later over on page 141 we'll dive into the history of the Hays Supermarket chain), but Taylor's was always a place to get a bite. Country stores often had a back counter and a kitchen, and you could pick up a sandwich to take with you when you picked up your bait for fishing or were heading out to the farm.

The 1983 opening of Taylor's included not only groceries but also sporting goods, bait, tackle and just about everything for living in rural Arkansas. It did so well that Chuck Taylor (Charles's son, who had by this time been working the grocery store for quite a while) opened a liquor store adjacent to Taylor's (local ordinances did not allow liquor stores and grocery stores to share the same building).

"My mother has always made barbecue. We've always done barbecue," Chuck Taylor told me. "You know, when the grocery store sales declined, we branched out and bought equipment and started doing hamburgers and po' boys and the lunch thing, sandwiches and fried fish, shrimp, oysters. Then it started to grow, so we started taking out grocery shelves, taking out sporting goods and adding tables and chairs for people to eat."

That little spot on the road from Dumas to Monticello started to pick up steam.

"We started out with two tables, and lunch just took over. We became full of tables. We still sold chips and drinks and stuff like that, knick-knacks," said Chuck. In fact, Taylor's cheese dip took on a great deal of notoriety, with people dropping by to pick up dip to take home. The restaurant even developed a big burger called the Double Bertha, which folks would try to eat in one setting.

But burgers weren't where the Taylors wanted to stop. Chuck and his wife, Pam, had plans.

It's always been our ambition to do a nighttime restaurant. So we started planning on it. We have a daughter in college now. We wanted to get her out of high school because she had activities at school—she was a majorette and we went to all the football games. We kinda held onto the lunch thing until we got her graduated. I perfected my recipes the whole time, for porterhouse steak, crawfish enchiladas, the whole time we knew we were going to do this.

Once we got her graduated, we let the liquor store license expire and took in the liquor store as part of the restaurant. We connected the two buildings, remodeled and started doing the night thing [in October 2012].

Chuck Taylor had worked out his dry-aging process over the years. While he'd always worked with the grocery and liquor stores, he made a living by supplementing with other jobs—as a cook in a duck lodge during fall and winter and surveying rice levies in spring and summer. "I started aging beef on a commercial scale when I worked a year at the Yellow Dog Lodge,"

Chuck shared, "I studied up on that while I was doing lunch, too. I got that perfected, I hope."

Taylor's steaks have quickly gained renown, not only for their flavor but also for their size. Kansas bone-in ribeyes and T-bone steaks run twenty-five to twenty-eight ounces. There's also a thirty-one- to thirty-five-ounce porterhouse steak for two. Once the day's supply is gone, they're out. There are other great dishes, such as that crawfish enchilada plate and two different lush versions of bread pudding. Of course, there's the cheese dip, too. "Our cheese dip is legendary. That's one of our claims to fame."

How does an upscale restaurant manage to make it in deep, rural Arkansas?

Anytime you step out of the loop of interest, as I told my wife Pam, you realize that you had to draw from a lot of different areas. You can't just make it on Dumas. The food has to be excellent. And it is, and we draw from everywhere—Little Rock, Texarkana, Mississippi, Fayetteville. The Panola people have come up from Louisiana. We've had a Saturday night where everyone in here was from DeWitt or Stuttgart. Pine Bluff, Monticello—you name it, people come, they love it, they say, "We will be back." That one person might tell ten people, and they come and they go tell ten people. Kinda like a chain letter, word of mouth is the best thing there is.

"It's kinda like *Field of Dreams*," Chuck told me, referencing the movie. "You build it, they will come. Yeah, it's a dream of mine to do this, but it might become a nightmare, too." He laughed at that. Something tells me with the great product he has and this growing restaurant, Chuck Taylor is going to be laughing all the way to the bank.

HARDIN FARMS, GRADY

I am glad that Hardin Farms and Market Too is located close to Little Rock in Scott, but the quiet old place in Grady seems a bit sad. It was once a lively location, with nearly year-round farm activities. Cars once filled the parking lot and lined U.S. Highway 65 at the old family farmstead.

It probably wasn't what Thomas Jefferson Hardin envisioned when he started the family farm in the nineteenth century. Back then, land around Grady was deeply forested in cypress, and it sold for just twenty cents an acre. T.J. Hardin's first business venture was taking in two hundred acres,

Hardin Farms in Grady. *Grav Weldon.*

then four hundred, and harvesting what happened to already be there. From there, he turned to cotton. He also turned to raising a family of five children. After his death, his wife, Betty, kept amassing more land and growing the farm.

Over the generations, the farm changed. In the 1940s, it was split between two brothers—one who embraced the mechanization of farm activity and the new chemicals and fertilizers available, the other who kept the old practices, crop rotation and hand-picking. Despite fire, drought and every other imaginable type of agricultural catastrophe, Hardin Farms continued to survive.

In the 1990s, Randy Hardin started planting cantaloupes, watermelons and pumpkins. One day, his daughter's daycare came out to see the pumpkin patch and pick their own. Seeing all the fun they were having gave him an idea. He started cutting a maze in the cornfield after the ears were harvested. Fresh produce and pecans were available for purchase. Soon, the farm was open for folks to stop by, experience life in the rural Delta and have a bite to eat. It became the site for an annual pilgrimage for city families wanting to share their agricultural background with their young. It also became a must-stop for travelers passing through southeast Arkansas.

Sadly, progress got in the way of that. In 2011, a bypass of Grady cut the farm in twain, and Hardin decided it wasn't safe to send kids across the new four-lane highway in wagons any more. The attraction was closed, and though the farms still produce, there's no stop at which to pick up vittles and no corn mazes to hide in any more. Grady itself has all but dried up, with the closing of its school and most of its population depleted.

However, on the third Thursday in August, there's a gathering that still brings the town to life. Politicians, food lovers and folks who trace their

The late M.E. Argo, a machinist and Grady Lions Club member, made the hush puppy machine in his welding shop more than a half century ago. The contraption, only used at the Grady Fish Fry, spits two dollops at a time into the hot grease. *Kat Robinson.*

ancestry to this Delta flat come to the annual Grady Fish Fry, hosted by the Lions Club as its major annual fundraiser. Approximately 1,400 tickets are sold each year. A dinner of fried catfish, hush puppies, French fries and watermelon is served under the sprawling old pecan trees in the Hardin yard. The Hardins even have a hush puppy machine, which tends to fascinate the Yankees.

The Hardin clan is still working hard to preserve farm life. Later on, I'll tell you what the Hardins are doing today in the community of Scott and the brother who's doing what he can to save farm life in the Delta.

THE LAST STRETCH TO PINE BLUFF

North on U.S. Highway 65, you start noticing more trees on the horizon to your left. The edges of Bayou Bartholomew demarcate the edge of the Delta and the start of the Timberlands. To the right, ponds and pools can be seen here and there; the Arkansas River is just over the levee in the distance.

Past Moscow and Noble Lake, you come to the southeastern edge of Pine Bluff. At the intersection of U.S. Highway 65 and Arkansas Highway 81, there's a long white building to the right. The east end is a convenience store; the west end is a restaurant that's survived more than sixty-five years.

Lavender's Barn began right after World War II, when a serviceman returning from overseas needed a new career. The restaurant was purchased and food was served. Not much has changed, though the décor was updated in the 1970s and seating seems to have been obtained from former fast-food restaurants. This is still a solid stop for patty melts, burgers, breakfasts and pie.

4
PINE BLUFF

In the early nineteenth century, European explorers anchored under a tall pine tree–laden bank along the Arkansas River. They named the area Pine Bluff. It's now the largest city in southeast Arkansas. Incorporated in 1839 with just fifty residents, the little port town grew to a major hub for agricultural and timber interests. Because of the Union forces that stationed there during the Civil War, it became a refuge for freemen and runaway slaves after the Emancipation Proclamation. After the war, the American Missionary Society worked with many of those families to establish the Branch Normal School of the Arkansas Industrial University, which later became the University of Arkansas–Pine Bluff, both the oldest black college and second oldest college in the state.

1873 saw the first rail line extended to the town, the same year that the Pine Bluff Gas Company started furnishing gas to light and heat homes. Cotton production and river commerce grew the town into Arkansas's third largest by 1890. By the end of the nineteenth century, the city had power and light, telephone service and streetcars.

Despite the Army Corps of Engineers building a levee on the opposite side of the Arkansas River, the river shifted, leaving an oxbow that became Lake Pine Bluff. The Great Flood of 1927 swamped the town and most of Jefferson County. There was progress, such as construction of the Saenger Theater in 1924, the opening of the Hotel Pines in 1913 and the first radio broadcast in Arkansas from local station WOK on February 18, 1922. In 1914, the Dollarway, a concrete road that connected Pine Bluff with the

Little Rock wagon trail at the Jefferson County line, was opened—reportedly costing a dollar per linear foot to construct.

New residents flooded in with the construction of Grider Field in April 1941 and the Pine Bluff Arsenal in December of that same year. Grider Field became a training ground and school for air force pilots, while chemical munitions were created and stored at the arsenal by the army.

With roads and the river to transport people to Pine Bluff, and jobs in agriculture and industry in abundance, the city's restaurant scene flourished. It reached a zenith in 1970, when 57,400 residents called it home. Unfortunately, the city has declined in the decades since. Between 2000 and 2010, the population fell from 55,085 to 49,083, a whopping 10 percent drop.

COLONIAL STEAKHOUSE, PINE BLUFF

The Tudor-style building at the corner of Eighth and Pine Streets started out as an elementary school back in 1912. After World War II, it served as a training facility for returning veterans, hence the garage. Today, it's home to a long-running restaurant.

Colonial Steakhouse began in an antebellum home at the corner of Fifth and Beech Streets, not too far away. It was the creation of a lady by the name of Mildred Compton, who opened it on August 10, 1973. She sold it to Scott Mouser, a twenty-two-year old local resident whose mom had once worked at the school housed in the current location. After a fire destroyed the Beech Street location in 1987, Mouser purchased the demolition rights for the Eighth and Pine Streets property and set about renovating. He moved the restaurant into the first floor and leased out the second for mortgage offices and such. He still owns the building today.

Mouser sold the restaurant to Joe and Donna Coker in 1993, and on June 3, 2014, the Cokers sold it to Dana and Wayne Gateley. Dana has been a waitress at Colonial Steakhouse for more than one-quarter of a century.

"The steakhouse has an amazing legacy of support," Dana told me when we chatted in early August 2014. "I have been brought to tears more times in the past month. Business people have come out in support, asking, 'What we can do for you,' 'How can we help?' Scott Mouser himself has gone to great expense to improve the building—the city has very strong restraints. And the eyes of the state and the nation are on us. We have been

Colonial Steakhouse is located in a century-old schoolhouse in downtown Pine Bluff. *Kat Robinson.*

fortunate—Scott has made sure all the problems have been addressed and the building has been kept up to date.

"We have the most amazing support, and we see the third generation of the same families. We do their prom [dinners] and engagement party and wedding reception. The kids come in the first time in high chairs and we see them through graduation and their wedding receptions."

Colonial Steakhouse is only open for dinner Tuesday through Saturday nights and never advertises for hires, since family members of staff come in when extra bodies are needed. Many staff members have other jobs. Some have been there forty years, and there have even been three generations of the same family working there at the same time.

"I went there as a favor to Scott and his wife," Dana shared, "they needed a waitress and I had owned a Baskin Robbins and I had no idea what I would do next after my kids graduated. I said I would help, and that's been some twenty years ago. I do work a day job, Scott owns the hunting club and a farm and his wife owns a pre-K through fifth grade school. Joe Coker is a vendor for Ben E. Keith, his wife is chairman of the math department at White Hall Schools.

"I think that maybe that has something to do with the success of the steakhouse. It has always been community-owned. Everyone has a steak at the Colonial, everyone in the community and customers from other cities like Conway, Little Rock, Beebe, Monticello and Dumas. On any particular Saturday night, we may have ten cities represented from fifty miles away, people coming in to celebrate anniversaries, birthdays, graduations. They always have—this is their special place, and because of that they consider us their restaurant."

When the Gateleys bought the eatery, Wayne Gateley asked if they should start taking reservations. The entire staff said no. "We can't tell a customer we're sorry, we're booked. They each have a special table, a special day of the week they come in. They would never understand that they'd need a reservation because it's their restaurant.

"I have a gentleman who celebrated a ninety-sixth birthday here the other day. I wait on his grandchildren. It's truly a legacy in Pine Bluff. Kids come in for prom that came in when they were a baby. I cannot tell you how many times I've had a young man tell me 'I'm going to propose Saturday night, what can we do to make it special?' Parents come in separately to take pictures of the proposal."

It's not just who eats there that defines the place. Colonial Steakhouse's menu has been knit together from the recommendations of its patrons and the suggestions of its staff. Veronica Scarver, who started working there when she was just fourteen years old, is responsible for the famed black bottom pie; her mother, Linda, came up with the famous Cotton Blossoms with apricot brandy sauce and the signature au gratin potatoes; her aunt Helen conjured the idea for the freshly cut salad bar. Dana Gateley has kept most of the recipes, adding lump crab cakes from Phillips Seafood in Baltimore and a dish of shrimp scampi over fettuccine. Those big steaks, though, will remain. Dana says:

We went for maybe our third or fourth anniversary back in the 1970s, my first time to Colonial Steakhouse. Someone told me, "You have to have the prime rib." I'm not much of a prime rib eater, but I did and then I was just onto it. It was a point where we were young and just starting out and it was two meals, and you had the other half the next day with carrots and potatoes and called it a roast.

Other restaurants take that standing seven bone rib, they take the rib out, cook the meat and then slice it and get twenty steaks out of it. We slice it into seven steaks and cook it directly over the fire. We don't pre-bake and slice it. That's why it doesn't have the leathery texture of most prime ribs. And it became one of the signature dishes, the Roast Prime of Beef, the monster. Businesspeople come in and they say to their clients, "There's not that much of it but it's really good" and we bring it out on a chain, dragging it from the kitchen.

On one visit, Grav and I ordered Cotton Blossoms, French onion soup, salad and bread and reserved some black bottom pie. Then out came my Roast Prime of Beef. Someone at another table actually whistled. The Internet, at least what was connected to my social media channels, blew up for a while over the enormity of it.

> The men's room at Colonial Steakhouse contains a very unusual and very large Roman-style urinal.

The Gateleys have made a few other recent changes, redecorating the restaurant in a Tuscan theme. They're leaving one room that will soon be decked out in photography of the city's restaurant past, a museum full of nostalgia for those generational customers who still keep coming back. Dana Gateley understands the restaurant's importance.

"It's hard to describe the history of it. The history [of the Colonial Steakhouse] is the history of the people of Pine Bluff. They are what made the history of the restaurant. It's like the knitting of the fabric—every string is a family, every strand is the history of this family. I have been asked why in the world I would buy the restaurant at my age. Well, I didn't buy it for me. I bought it for the families."

SNO-WHITE GRILL, PINE BLUFF

The Colonial is far from the oldest place in town still operating. That honor goes to the Sno-White Grill. Originally opened in 1936, it's become well known for its sloppy burgers and housemade pies.

Ownership has changed a few times over the years—as you'd expect from a seventy-eight-year-old restaurant. The last change came in 1970, when Roy Marshall sold the place to Bobby Garner, who's still running it today. Within its wood-clad walls you'll find every manner of individual, just stopping in for a meal and perhaps some gossip.

The waitresses are savvy, and they'll be honest with you about the food. I've gone before and been warned away from the gravy when it wasn't perfect or directed to an appropriate dessert. The meals are simple, and the burgers are the best in town.

There are two named burgers—the Hutt and the Perdue. The latter is named for the long-standing printing company in town, while the former's

The Sno-White Grill in Pine Bluff dates back to 1936. *Grav Weldon.*

Rich's Hamburgers opened in 1987 on Walnut on the northwest side of downtown in a little orange-enhanced building. The gutbomb burgers cost less than a buck and come swimming in liquid gold—er, molten grease. Rich's also sells foot-long hot dogs and legendary hot ham and cheese sandwiches. It's cash-only, Monday through Friday. *Grav Weldon.*

namesake is the Hutt Building Material Company. Both are within spitting distance of the shop.

The reason behind the name of the restaurant is lost to time; however, the Disney film with a similar name opened in 1937, a full year after the Sno-White Grill made it into the phone book.

CATFISH IN PINE BLUFF

Being on the banks of the Arkansas River, Pine Bluff has more than its share of catfish lovers. They come out to restaurants and swarm en mass, a feeding frenzy of diners searching out cornmeal-covered catfish, breaded, deep fried and served with sweet hush puppies. In Jefferson County, few catfish-centric eateries fail to reach the standard.

Amongst the many people who have called Pine Bluff home, Gilbert Maxwell "Bronco Billy" Anderson (1880–1971) may be the best known. Born in Little Rock, Max Aronson grew up in Pine Bluff before moving to New York to appear in the first western movie production, *The Great Train Robbery*, in 1903. He changed his professional name before starring in over four hundred "Bronco Billy" movies.

Arnold's Catfish in Pine Bluff. *Grav Weldon.*

Of these many dives, Arnold's Catfish Kitchen is perhaps the best known. Open since 1973, the lowslung white building on Blake Street, not far from Kibb's Bar-B-Que (I'll tell you about that on page 81), is often smelled rather than sighted by passersby, during cooking hours. It's not fancy, but it is a magnificent place to get your meat-and-three. Catfish is the star, but the hot rolls are legendary.

Down on Camden Road just past Exit 39 off Interstate 530, you'll find Leon's Catfish and Seafood. Another long-lived place, Leon's is known for rather thin and thinly breaded but crisp catfish filets; the vinegary coleslaw and the fat hushpuppies laced with jalapeños and served with cheese dip make it memorable.

BIG BANJO

Richard "Dickey" Ratliff opened up the first Big Banjo pizza restaurant in Pine Bluff in 1973, and the original location is still open today. You may have seen other Big Banjos around. He's responsible for them, too. Back in the 1970s, pizza got hot and popular in Arkansas. While drive-ins and diners were still popular, the pizza joint became a great place to socialize, especially for teenagers and families. While in other areas of Arkansas big chains like Pizza Inn and Pizza Hut moved in, Big Banjo started up in Pine Bluff.

The Big Banjo in Pine Bluff.
Grav Weldon.

Dickey Ratliff opened the first location in 1973 in Pine Bluff and then two more locations before branching out to Stuttgart, Malvern and Dumas (and adding another Pine Bluff location). Today, he's sold most of the locations off, but he still owns the original location in Pine Bluff and leases out the Dumas location. Today you can still get the same good old supreme or taco pizza beloved by generations of hungry patrons.

LYBRAND'S BAKERY

The oldest bakery in Pine Bluff is also the oldest left in the Arkansas Delta. Back in 1940, Curtis Lybrand was working for a dairy company in the city. After he married his wife, Emma Jean, the two decided to go into the bakery business. They opened Lybrand's Bakery with $300 in seed money and a ton of enthusiasm along the 100 block of Main Street in 1946. That place didn't take, so six months later they went to a spot in East Harding. They moved to another Main Street location another six months later. This one seemed to stick, and it's at 1308 Main Street that Lybrand's Bakery really began to take hold.

In the early days, it was cakes and doughnuts that brought business through the door. It didn't take long for Danish pastries, pies, coffee cakes, yeast rolls and bread to be added to the mix. Eventually they started making wedding cakes, and a Lybrand's wedding cake became *the* cake for high-class nuptials in town. In 1965, a second location was opened.

Today, Lybrand's Bakery is operated by Joey and Marcia Lybrand, with two locations—one on Hazel Street and one on Dollarway Road. It's much more than a bakery now, with a full breakfast served in the mornings and sandwiches and lunch specials in the afternoons. But it's the doughnuts that keep people coming back—pliant golden rings, light and dark twists and even cinnamon rolls.

IRISH MAID, PINE BLUFF AND FORT SMITH

Irish Maid traces its lineage back to two brothers, Frank and Jim Claghorn, who lived in Little Rock. The brothers baked doughnuts and sold them door to door. Frank ended up moving to Fort Smith, where he started Irish Maid

It's hard to miss Irish Maid Donuts in Pine Bluff. *Grav Weldon.*

Donuts in 1960. Jim moved to Pine Bluff and started up the identically named shop in 1961.

At first, both made every one of their items by hand, from the famed maple bars to apricot fillings to the decadent Bavarian cream. Eventually both of them hired help. They both married, too. Today, the Fort Smith shop is run by the Adairs—Frank's daughter's kids.

Jim ran the Pine Bluff shop until 1988, when he finally sold to a couple who had worked with him some time, Steve and Cheryl Grinstead. The two are the shop's only employees; they start each evening at 10:00 p.m. and work through until 10:00 a.m. the next day, or whenever they run out of pastries.

The shop is small, but it has its share of regulars who have been coming in at least once a week for decades. The vanilla cream–filled doughnuts are marvelous, and in my humble opinion, there is no finer maple bar in the state.

COUNTRY KITCHEN, PINE BLUFF

Pine Bluff has seen its share of classic eateries, from chains such as Burger Chef, Minute Man, Bowen's, AQ Chicken House and Coffee Cup to homegrown favorites such as the Embers, King Kat, the Midget, Norton's Cafeteria, Moretti's Italian Restaurant, the White Cottage Café and the Wagon Wheel. All are gone, thanks to progress and change. But Country Kitchen abides.

Situated on the northwest side of town, once hailed as the most modern restaurant in town, the old brown diner manages to hang on. The place serves up barbecue, plate lunches, breakfasts and more.

Unusually, there's another option to salad or fries with your dinner—deviled eggs. In fact, the little diner has become known for those bite-sized swallows, served in pairs. Not a lot of folks are doing deviled eggs on the restaurant scene, so this is an extra bonus. Oh, and there's pie.

THE TRIO CLUB, PINE BLUFF

Just a few blocks down and on the other side of the road, there's a sign for a local lodge. That sign used to proudly proclaim the location of the Trio Club, a joint once owned by Floyd and Birdie Brown. The Browns moved to Jefferson County in the 1930s, where Floyd worked at a sawmill. The Browns' oldest daughter, Maxine, started singing early, and they encouraged her. They also built the Trio Club as a nightclub on the west side of town. Maxine and her brother Jim Ed became a duo, singing in different towns across the region and ending up on the *Barnyard Frolic*, a live weekly radio show, in 1952.

The Trio Club, run by the Brown family, was a favorite haunt of Elvis Presley. *Courtesy Maxine Brown.*

The Brown kids hadn't planned on musical careers, but Maxine's songwriting and Jim Ed's singing talents changed that after she penned "Looking Back To See," a novelty duet released in 1954. Younger sister Bonnie joined soon afterward, adding a third harmony part. "Looking Back To See" went to number eight on the charts. Their next song, "Here Today and Gone Tomorrow," which Maxine also wrote, went to number seven. Initially billed as "Jim Edward, Maxine & Bonnie Brown," by 1958, they were performing and recording simply as "the Browns."

They joined *The Louisiana Hayride* in 1954, where they met and befriended Elvis Presley, who was seeking a job on the show. The Browns toured with Presley from 1954 to 1956, when they became members of the nationally broadcast TV series, *The Ozark Jubilee.*

In 1959, the Browns released the record that would make them world-famous, "The Three Bells," an English version of the French song "Les Trois Cloches." Their producer was the renowned guitarist Chet Atkins. The song went to number one on the country music charts and stayed there for ten weeks. It topped the pop charts for four weeks, and it even went to number ten on the rhythm and blues chart. After that, the Browns "crossed over" from the country to the pop charts with "Scarlet Ribbons," "The Old Lamplighter" and "Send Me the Pillow You Dream On." The group joined the Grand Ole Opry in 1963.

But I was going to tell you about the Trio Club, and Maxine Brown can certainly tell you about that. She wrote a marvelous book a few years ago called, appropriately enough, *Looking Back To See*. Brown's friendship with Elvis Presley is well-known; she often speaks to groups about their affiliation. And she'll tell you, he was always a gentleman.

I used to do all the laundry for us. We would save all our nickles and dimes for the washeteria. I tried doing only one load, as it would be too [expensive] for two machines. One time, I happened to throw in a pair of my red silk panties. I know I had seen my mom wash them a hundred times in the past. But this time, everything came out pink, all the boys' undershorts, shirts and socks. Everyone was upset. Everyone that is, except Elvis. He loved the color pink, as everyone knows. I told the guys, "Don't worry, when we get to Tyler, I will have Billie Perryman show me how to bleach and we will get those things back white again."

Tom and Billie Perryman were our friends and they were the ones who booked us together off the Louisiana Hayride. Back in those days, Elvis was paid $100 a day, and out of that he paid Scotty and Bill $25 each. The Browns were paid $125 a day. The three of us liked to eat high on the hog, therefore none of us ever had any money.

Billie helped me get the boys belongings back white again. Elvis refused to let me bleach his shorts, shirts or socks. He said, "I want them to stay this color." He wore those socks for a whole month. He was afraid if I washed them, they would fade. They got to smelling so bad that someone—I think it was Scotty Moore—caught him asleep and took those socks and threw them out the car window, along with his shoes.

We got way on down the road (from where we had been staying), and Elvis was mad. Scotty assured him that we would stop at the next department store and buy him some new socks and shoes. It was Sunday and we had a show that night. I told Scotty, "You won't be buying anything today; everything will be closed." Back then, we had what was called "The Blue Law," which prohibited Sunday sales of certain merchandise. All of the department stores would be closed. You couldn't buy a pair of shoes of socks to save your life.

Scotty said, "Well, the only solution is, go back and find those shoes and socks." Nobody would ever believe this, but he drove right to them. Even the buzzards wouldn't touch those things. Elvis did the show that night with those stinking shoes and socks!

The next day Scotty and Bill found him some new shoes but no pink socks. I said, "I bet he wouldn't know the difference if we bought him some pink girl socks." Sure enough, we found some and bought every pair the store had. We all split the cost, only too happy to do so. Sometimes that smell was just too much for us hillbillies.

Bill Black found some silk polka dot undershorts. He thought he would play a joke on Elvis and buy him these boxer shorts, as he never seemed to have any clean shorts. The joke backfired, Elvis loved those shorts and refused to let me wash them. So, the boys had to find another men's store and find him some more silk underpants. They were not able to find the polka dot ones but Elvis didn't care as long as they were silk. Elvis never let cotton touch his skin after this. Eventually he let me wash his underclothes. I always wondered why he never had any. Only Elvis knew the answer to this question.

Okay, once again, I've strayed from the story. But now you know something about The King's underpants.

The Trio Club gained a lot of popularity, and it was one of the great places to listen to good music. Lots of well-known country musicians passed through over the years, including Conway Twitty, Jim Reeves, the Louvin Brothers, Ray Price and Porter Wagner. Birdie Brown's southern-style cooking became well known, and she got a reputation for perfectly interpreting the area's cuisine, whether it was tomato gravy or turkey steaks, country-fried ham with red eye gravy and biscuits, corn fritters or coconut cream pie. And then there's banana pudding, which Maxine Brown says was Elvis's favorite. She kindly shared this recipe.

Mama Brown's Banana Pudding

4 eggs, whole or separated (if using whites for meringue)
2½ cups sugar
2 Tablespoons cornstarch
1 large can (12 ounces) Pet condensed milk
2 tablespoons vanilla
Dash of salt
1 stick (8 tablespoons) butter

1 box (12 ounces) vanilla wafers
5–6 bananas, sliced
1 cup whipping cream
2 tablespoons sugar

Beat the eggs until foamy; add 2½ cups of sugar and the cornstarch. Mix well and then add milk, vanilla and salt. Cook in a double boiler until the mixture thickens. Remove from heat. Pour a layer into the bottom of pudding pan. Add a layer of vanilla wafers and bananas until all used up. Combine the whipping cream and 2 tablespoons of sugar. Whip until fluffy. Top the pie with whipped cream (if you are topping with a meringue, skip the whipped cream).

Brown shared one more note about Elvis Presley on that pudding: "My mom always made this for him. If Scotty and Bill were with him, she made sure the recipe was doubled, or tripled."

Mammoth Orange Café, Redfield

If you stay on Arkansas Highway 365 heading northwest out of Pine Bluff, you'll reach the last destination along this stretch. It's in Redfield, and trust me, you cannot beat the Mammoth Orange Café.

Ernestine Bradshaw opened the original round orange building on June 1, 1965. She had lived in California before moving to Arkansas

The Mammoth Orange Café was designed to resemble the famous Frank E. Pohl orange juice stands of California. The cinder block addition was attached later. *Grav Weldon.*

and was inspired to have a small dairy stand such as the many she'd seen there. Most of the orange stands she had found in California were either built by or inspired by the creations of Frank E. Pohl, who opened his first orange-shaped stand in 1926.

Singular in Arkansas, the Mammoth Orange Café eventually grew with the addition of a cinder block structure at its rear to accommodate dine-in customers. Ms. Ernestine ran the restaurant until her death in 2007. Her daughter, Cynthia Carter, runs it today. The menu is a bit more broad now (a full kitchen was part of the addition), including hamburger steak with gravy, burgers and chicken sandwiches, catfish on Fridays and, of course, ice cream delights. If you go, take cash; the Mammoth Orange Café has never taken credit or debit.

5
STUTTGART

Our circumnavigation of the Lower Delta on the Great River Road and U.S. Highway 65 covers a lot of ground, but it misses an integral town within the region; a burg especially important for its dual role as the Duck and Rice Capital of the World. Of course, I'm talking about Stuttgart. The heart of the Grand Prairie lies at the crossroads of U.S. Highways 63, 79 and 165. It's forty-five minutes from Pine Bluff, an hour from Marianna and about forty-five minutes from Brinkley.

The town was founded by German immigrant George Adam Buerkle, a Lutheran minister who arrived in Ohio in 1852. In 1878, he purchased seven thousand acres on the vast expanse in the heart of the Arkansas Delta and recruited a colony of forty-eight men, women and children to the site. The next year, he brought in the second colony, which included his family. All of the land he didn't keep for himself, he sold to the new residents at the same price he'd paid—just three dollars an acre. He named the new community after his German hometown.

Stuttgart didn't really take off until the late 1880s, when the railroad was first pushed up from Gillett to the south. It was incorporated in 1889, and its first mayor was Colonel Robert Crockett, the grandson of the famed frontiersman Davy Crockett. The area's industry focused on furniture making, wagons, blacksmithing, woodworking and farm implements. Several dairies and even a soft drink plant were established there.

The town's destiny blossomed in 1902, when Bill Hope planted the first plot of rice as an experiment. Even though folks kept "sampling" the plot for souvenir rice plants, it produced wildly—139 bushels per acre. Rice took off in the area; and the Stuttgart Rice Mill Company was incorporated in 1907. In 1921, a band of farmers formed a cooperative and created what is now Riceland Foods, the world's largest miller and marketer of rice. A second company, Producers Rice Mill, was established in 1943 and continues to also produce impressively.

The city quickly expanded during World War II with the government's purchase of a large number of rice fields north of town and the establishment of an airbase. In addition to using Stuttgart-area rice to feed troops, the airbase housed German prisoners of war during the conflict.

Today, the town still boasts a population of nearly ten thousand—a number that increases two- to five-fold each November as duck season opens.

Sportsmans' Drive-In in Stuttgart. *Grav Weldon.*

In 1936, the Wings Over the Prairie Festival was created to celebrate ducks and duck hunting, and today it's host to the annual World Championship Duck Calling Competition, which draws in competitors from all over the world. Private duck lodges bustle throughout the fall and winter months, while farming is the focus of spring and summer.

Stuttgart has a collection of classic restaurants and such lost to time. The most famous of these might be Little Chef. Run by LeiAnn and Bill Holbert inside a little Quonset hut on Michigan Street, it was a welcoming place where you could always find a good meal and some of the best chicken and dumplings ever created. After LeiAnn's death in 2008 and the destruction of the location for a bypass, Little Chef was never rebuilt.

There was the Pam Pam Club, which was a members-only supper club that opened in 1952, where you could order up a steak and eat—and drink!—like a king.

There are still places to get good pie in town, most notably Dew-Baby's for egg custard and Pat's Place for coconut and chocolate meringue. The bowling alley has a pretty good burger. But none of those places can be considered classic under the twenty years guideline.

What can be? Well, if you're craving a burger, you have to venture into the Sportsman's Drive-In. It's not a drive-in; it's more of a joint, a greasy spoon, a scary looking place to spend your lunch money. Don't let the old aluminum building in the middle of that flat gravel parking lot under the ancient Schlitz sign scare you. Within, you'll discover a bevy of treasures, from the almost-too-well-spiced catfish to the pooled-jus-on-top ribeye steak. What you really want to eat here comes for $6.59—an eleven-ounce cheeseburger with all the fixings, served up with hand-cut fries. Just don't tell your cardiologist.

KIBB'S BAR-B-QUE

Then there's barbecue. Barbecue in Arkansas comes beef or pork, smoked or "qued," as the menu will tell you, unless you want to dig further down into your country roots and have a barbecued bologna sandwich. Doesn't really matter—as long as you get to Kibb's Bar-B-Que, because as the sign says, "Today is a Good Day for 'Bar-B-Que!'"

The original opened at Second and Buerkle Streets around 1980, under the eye of Emmajean and Walter Kibble. It seems they had a falling out at

Kibb's Bar-B-Que #2 in Stuttgart. *Grav Weldon.*

some point along the way, and he took off for Pine Bluff—where he started the second Kibb's Bar-B-Que.

Walter ended up coming back to town and opening up Kibb's #2 Bar-B-Que (even though it's actually the third location) over on Park Avenue at Harrison Street. Today, all the Kibb's Bar-B-Ques are still going strong (along with a Grand Kibb's Bar-B-Que in North Little Rock, run by the grandkids). Go in, have a sandwich and some of their marvelous slaw (both on the bun and on the side) and a cold beer, if that's your thing.

The one thing to note about both Sportsman's Drive-In and Kibb's Bar-B-Que is that they don't take your credit card. Bring cash, bring an appetite and, especially during duck season, bring your patience—both places will be overflowing.

DUCK GUMBO

Back to Wings Over the Prairie. This annual celebration the week of Thanksgiving swells the town to bursting. It's a homecoming for the city and a pilgrimage for the most serious of duck hunters. There are celebrations of all sort, shopping you'll never find anywhere else (especially at the enormous, popular Mack's Prairie Wings) and a unique culture where every girl wears jeans, jackets and boots. In fact, on my first visit I was the lone holdout wearing sneakers amongst thousands that crowded downtown.

And then there's Duck Gumbo. Back in my TV days, I can recall hearing just a scant mention of it from fellow producer Rebecca Buerkle and I'd heard whispers about it, but when I agreed to cover celebration for the first time, I thought I was simply writing about a cooking competition. I truly had no idea what I would encounter in the giant tent that took up a football field's space on the lot of Producers Rice Mill on U.S. Highway 165. Grav and I arrived that Saturday, showed our IDs and were tagged with wristbands before we proceeded into the mass of humanity beyond.

The competitors each have their own booths, and in those booths they have to come up with a suitable gumbo in just a few hours, consisting of half duck and half whatever else they serve up. Those booths can be anything from a couple tables and a banner to stories-tall duck blind structures complete with viewing decks on top, often with ladies in skimpy clothes or guys in funny hats throwing beads into the crowd. The décor fell between Razorback football ultrafandom to duck hunter's delight to taxidermy havoc to, well, anything.

Early on it was very relaxed, a couple hundred people flitting between different stands, chatting with others and nibbling cheese and crackers, sausages and such. One booth had quartered pork barbecue sandwiches, another sausage balls and spinach dip, another salami and olive appetizers

Hundreds converge in a tent for the annual Duck Gumbo cook off at the Wings Over the Prairie Festival in downtown Stuttgart. *Grav Weldon.*

on skewers, another beef and bean chili. Between those were croissant-wrapped Lil' Smokies and cheese balls with Fritos; there were competitors hovering over pots, every different color of roux cooking, from deep brown to bright red to pale green.

And then there were the scents. The lovely smoky scent of sausage and the wild bite of duck combined with all sorts of things—okra, celery, tomatoes, bell peppers, onions and spices—slightly different at each stand, but still always with that prevalent scent of the main ingredient underneath. Duck was getting its due in those pots.

A gentleman from one booth came up to me with a tissue, which he quickly and quietly tucked into my cleavage. I started to issue a protest but he held up a spray gun of water, shot me at the collarbone with it and pressed something to my chest. "This is your first time here, ain't it?" he asked me.

"Sure is."

"You stick out like a sore thumb, but that's okay. You look like a box of crayons. That's good." He pulled away the thing against my chest and pulled the tissue out of my shirt. "What do you think?"

I looked down and saw he'd applied a tie dyed peace sign temporary tattoo. I grinned. "That's pretty good."

"I hope I got it right side up. You have a good time."

The next booth's purveyor adorned me with beads. I'd been told that the event was considered "redneck Mardi Gras," but having experienced Mardi Gras, I figured it was a bit too light for that. Huh. About three-quarters of the way around my survey of the place, I got smacked on the butt. I turned around to see a couple of guys laughing.

"Oh, she's a noob!" one of them laughed. I smiled and moved on, thinking it was a random incident. It was not. Over the next couple of hours I got smacked numerous times. It was like some sort of fraternity rite, but instead of leaving stinging cheeks, these rascals were leaving stickers, a lot of stickers.

And was this frowned upon? Not at all. In fact, many of the local girls (all in the "uniform" of tight jeans, camoflauge jacket and knee-high boots) were showing off their sticker-bedazzled bottoms. I ran into an old friend, Josh Heffington, who had his cell phone out, showing off photos from last year's debacle, random bottoms plastered from one hip to the other with a smattering of stickers. Apparently it's a source of pride.

As the afternoon progressed, smoke hung in the air and the crowd packed in. The hired band started playing between updates from the Razorback game. There were lines at the liquor stands. Groups of older men and groups of teens were chewing the fat and having a good time. It reminded me of a

Jimmy Buffett party on a beach. The competition came second to the party. Grav managed to talk one of the guys manning a booth near the epicenter of the event into letting him up on the upper platform. He told me later how the platform swayed.

At three o'clock the cooking was over and the judging began. Booth after booth was prepared for the big moment. And then the floodgates were open for anyone to try. Each participant is required to cook at least three quarts of gumbo, but most of the competitors I saw made gallons, and they were generous with samples. A host of six-ounce Styrofoam cups appeared like egrets on Lake Conway, each with its own sample of a different duck gumbo. Some included tasso, andouille, ham, pork chops or summer sausage, even possum.

Of course, this was all going on at the same time as the World Championship Duck Calling Competition, which we felt compelled to check out. To our surprise, though, the vendor tents along Main Street were packed and we left Duck Gumbo at a point of standing-room-only, there were less than one hundred in the crowd watching the contest.

We realized why mere minutes later. Each competitor has ninety seconds to do five calls. They are, for all intents and purposes, the same five calls. And while I'm somewhat used to duck calls, it about drove Grav out of his head. The idea of sitting through it all was just too much.

If you go to Wings Over the Prairie, you'll probably want to spend a few minutes watching the duck calling. You'll certainly want to check out the vendor booths. But if you're an adult and you like "a good time," you really should be over in the parking lot at Producers Rice Mill under the big tent. It's unforgettable.

Duck Gumbo

1 stick (8 tablespoons) butter, divided into 2 tablespoons and 6 tablespoons
4 wild-harvested ducks or 2 domestic ducks, fully dressed
2 tablespoons salt
1 cup all-purpose flour
1 cup chicken broth
1½ cups onion, chopped
1½ cups celery, chopped
1½ cups green bell pepper, chopped
3 cloves garlic, minced

1 clove garlic, smashed
1 bay leaf
1 pound smoked beef or pork sausage or Andouille
1 tablespoon black pepper
1 tablespoon cayenne pepper
1 tablespoon garlic pepper sauce
Gumbo file powder to taste
Rice

In a wide skillet, heat 1 tablespoon ($1/8$ stick) of butter. Rub ducks with salt. Place in skillet and sear until nicely browned. Remove ducks to a large stockpot, leaving behind drippings. Add remainder of the stick of butter. Over high heat, whisk together melted butter and drippings with flour until it forms a roux that is chestnut to chocolate brown in color and pasty. Immediately remove from heat and add chicken broth; continue to whisk until roux is fully incorporated. Add to stockpot along with the vegetables, all of the garlic and the bay leaf. Add just enough water to cover duck, then put on the lid and let it simmer for two hours.

Slice sausage and add to pot with cayenne and black peppers and garlic pepper sauce. Cover and simmer for 30 minutes. Taste and adjust seasoning by adding salt, pepper or more garlic pepper sauce. Let simmer, stirring occasionally for up to four hours. Serve with gumbo file over rice.

Part Two

THE UPPER DELTA

6

ROCK 'N' ROLL HIGHWAY 67

To the south of Little Rock at the heart of the state, there's the first roll of the Ouachitas and the wooded sections of timber all the way to Pine Bluff. South from there, Bayou Bartholomew's run down to the Louisiana border gives a neat line to delineate the Lower Delta from points westerly.

North of Little Rock, there's more of a blending of the Ozark's last rolling hills with the sometimes swampy, sometimes forested edges of the Grand Prairie. Once you get to Searcy, where U.S. Highway 67 crosses the Little Red River, the separation is more defined. The four-lane expressway rolls over a few languishing hills into Bald Knob before paralleling the last low ridge of the Ozarks up to Newport. The old highway, still demarcated as U.S. Highway 67 for now but destined to join other old highway sections as Arkansas Highway 367 in the future, keeps that ridge in view all the way to Pocahontas, where it skirts that ridge by a block before heading northeast to Corning and out into Missouri.

U.S. Highway 67 is as good a line as any to note the end of the Delta's reach and what I use here to separate it from the Ozarks. There are a few places between this line and the limit of what I covered in *Classic Eateries of the Ozarks and Arkansas River Valley*, and I'll share those in the final section of this book.

U.S. Highway 67 was created in 1926 along with the bones of the initial federal highway system, over the route of the original Southwest Trail that lead frontiersmen from St. Louis to Texas. Its original route from Fredericktown, Missouri, to Dallas, Texas, has been extended; the

Texas route goes to Presidio and becomes Mexican Federal Highway 16 on the other side of the Rio Grande, while the north end now terminates at Sabula, Iowa. In southern Arkansas it follows most of its original path with exceptions around Donaldson and between Benton and Little Rock. North of Pulaski County, its original alignment lies mostly along Arkansas Highway 367, which runs east of the current U.S Highway 67 expressway to Searcy before crossing through the heart of town and up along the edge of the Ozarks to just south of Swifton, where the abrupt end of the expressway is tied back to the original highway via a two-lane highway. The White River runs between the two sections south of Newport for several miles.

Plans are to eventually expand the expressway all the way to the Missouri border; however, the state's lack of plans to tie in the expressway to its northern line has left little hurry to getting the rest of the job done. A lone expressway section in Walnut Ridge loops trucks around the city from U.S. Highway 63.

There is a section remaining of the original U.S. Highway 67 pavement, which dates back to 1929, between Alicia and Hoxie. You'll often see people fishing from bridges along the stretch during the warmer months.

Who Dat's, Bald Knob

Bald Knob is a good place to start when you're talking about the Upper Delta. Situated at the intersection of U.S. Highways 64, 67 and 167, it's also at the foot of the first rolling hills of the Ozarks. Set off north along U.S. Highway 167, and the roads quickly begin to curl and bob along the first ridges. Head east along U.S. Highway 64, and it's a straight-flat roll all the way to West Memphis with just a few hops over rivers and swings around old downtowns. Go south and you race through wooded lands to Little Rock.

Before heading north, there are three restaurants to mention. The first is the old Kelley's Restaurant, which has family ties to an existing operation in Wynne and a now-closed restaurant in Batesville. The second ties in with the first. It owes its origins to several things, including a fading southern Louisiana oil industry, a failed start-up business and Kelley's.

It all started with Doug Stelly. Back in southern Louisiana, in a little place called Abbieville, the young man learned to cook when he was seven and grew up immersed in Cajun cookery. As a young adult, he worked his way up from dishwasher to manager of an Abbieville steakhouse and then

Who Dat's Cajun Restaurant in Bald Knob. *Grav Weldon.*

started his own eatery. When the oil business dried up around the area, his restaurant dried up, too.

Fortuitously, a Bald Knob restaurant owner passing through the area got Stelly's name and asked him to come up to Arkansas to keep the place going. It didn't work out, and Stelly was back to square one.

It didn't take long being back in Louisiana for Stelly to realize that Bald Knob was the place he really wanted to be, so he headed back north and took a job with Sam Kelley at Kelley's Restaurant. A short time later, Stelly and his wife, Sam, bought a hamburger stand and had their own restaurant.

What they discovered, though, was that people in Bald Knob had liked the Cajun cooking from that other restaurant operation and they wanted it back. Unable to get financing, the couple cleared out the backyard and built an eatery right onto the back of their house. Thus in 1992, Who Dat's was born.

The restaurant has expanded several times, but still, on Friday and Saturday nights you'll see people camped out around the porch and picnic tables in the parking lot, waiting for a chance to get in, for good reason. The crawfish etouffee, fried frog legs, gumbo and every other item comes from old family recipes. The Stellys' five kids and even both their mothers have been involved in the operation.

When you see all those folks patiently waiting for a chance to get inside the doors to a table for blackened catfish, fried shrimp and jambalaya, it's hard to believe that Who Dat's doesn't advertise. It's all word-of-mouth, and fortunately for Doug and Sam Stelly and their kin, it's been good.

When you go, be ready to wait. If you have a big appetite or just want to graze, have yourself the Food Bar—a combination salad station and Sunday-style potluck that includes white rice, red beans and rice with sausage, smothered chicken with Creole spices, butterbeans cooked with tomatoes, corn on the cob, blackeyed peas, green beans with bacon, barbecue baked beans, home fries, carrots, English peas, baked chicken and corn off the cob. Of course, that's entirely sidestepping the fantastically prepared seafood and Cajun and Creole favorites, but it's the cheap choice and a good feast.

THE BULLDOG DRIVE IN, BALD KNOB

The third restaurant in Bald Knob is usually at the top of travelers' lists, especially late in the spring. The Bulldog Drive In was opened in 1978 by Bob Miller, who raised the money for his fledgling enterprise by working summers during high school and college on a pipeline. He spent his first two years after college working on the Transatlantic Alaskan Pipeline. Other restaurants had operated in the building where he constructed his dream; they'd all failed, but Miller was determined to succeed. He even took on the name of the last restaurant that tried to make it there. The Bulldog, after all, refers to the Bald Knob high school mascot. Miller's wife, Lece, worked there when she was in high school.

It wasn't easy in the beginning, but the restaurant did eventually develop a following of local folks who were thrilled with a reasonably priced drive-in that offered pit barbecue, burgers and cheap plate-lunch specials.

However, out-of-towners make the special stop in through the late spring and summer months because of a very special item—the restaurant's famed strawberry shortcake. This isn't a fluffy pound cake version, and it's not served on biscuits like many Arkansas home cooks do it. Miller's grandmother's recipe is still used to make the shortcake, which is rolled out and baked. It's thin, and it's served covered in fresh strawberries and their juices. You can have it with whipped cream, nuts and even ice cream. But

The Bulldog Drive In in Bald Knob. *Gray Weldon.*

you can't have it in the fall and winter. Miller uses mostly local berries but stretches the season a little if he can get fresh berries from within the United States. Typically that means you can get the delightful dessert between April Fool's Day and Labor Day.

RHYTHM ROAD

In 2009, the Arkansas legislature, through Act 497, designated 111 miles of the original U.S. Highway 67 as Rock 'N' Roll Highway 67 through Jackson, Lawrence, Randolph and Clay Counties. This stretch of the highway was the site of numerous juke joints, roadhouses, theaters and dives between the end of the Second World War and the 1980s. The last of these, the King of Clubs, burned in 2010. Elvis Presley performed there, as did Johnny Cash, who once got up and sang three songs for twenty dollars on the stage inside the undistinguished white building near Swifton.

The others—including the King's Capri, Sunset Inn, Bloody Bucket, 67 Club, Sunset Inn, Jarvis's and Silver Moon—were incubators for a whole new line of American music. It's where many early rock-and-roll stars first cut their teeth. In addition to Presley and Cash, other acts such as Jerry Lee Lewis, Sonny Burgess, Billy Lee Riley and Conway Twitty sang their hearts out and tried new tunes in front of those crowds. Notes of blues, gospel and even country blended together with the fledgling rock sound to produce another of Arkansas's native forms—rockabilly, a term created by crossing rock with hillbilly.

The long stretch of pavement tying the miles together offered a quick route to musical bliss for decades. Today, the joints themselves are celebrated at Newport's Rock 'N' Roll Highway 67 Museum.

Smokehouse BBQ and Lackey's Tamales, Newport

I've already shared the origins of the Arkansas Delta tamale, and of the chicken-fat-and-beef creations made by Ms. Rhoda Adams in Lake Village. There is yet a third set of tamales that you should consider when crisscrossing the Delta. Those would be the Cajun-style chicken-filled maize rolls known as Lackey's Tamales.

Mind you, if you start looking around Newport for a restaurant called Lackey's, you're not going to find it. The eatery that bore the name and

Smokehouse BBQ in Newport. *Grav Weldon.*

a sign out front that proclaimed, "Lackey's Cajun Style Hot Tamales" is gone. Fortunately there's still one bastion of spicy tamale goodness out there: a little restaurant on the south side of town, a diminutive place called Smokehouse BBQ.

We went on a stormy Friday night in March 2014. It was packed. We were told to go find a seat, and a waitress brought out a thick menu with every sort of Southern delight on it—a full slate of breakfast; barbecue plates of chopped beef, pork and pork ribs; Cajun and steak plates featuring Omaha steaks; tamale plates loaded with chili and cheese; Cajun staples of red beans and rice, gumbo and jambalaya; catfish and shrimp plates with lobster tail and crab leg add-ons; lunch and dinner specials and Happy Hour specials; chicken plates and salads and gator bites; burgers and po' boys and a Philly cheesesteak. Amidst the appetizers, a bright orange block proclaimed, "Lackey's Tamales, Cajun-Style chicken tamales wrapped in cornhusk," with one, six or twelve in an order.

Grav had never had a Lackey's tamale before, and his fondness for Rhoda's and Pasquale's tamales kept his excitement down. He was interested in the Cajun cheese dip and got it, but I got a word in and asked the waitress to bring him just one. She admitted to me a heresy—she doesn't eat tamales, since her dad used to eat the sort out of a can (the *shame*), but knew they were good. She retrieved the ordered items while we decided on dinner.

We had just about decided to split a big barbecue combo plate between the two of us when she set the tamale down in front of him and, after photographing the thing, Grav took a timid bite. Then it was gone. He even changed his order (leaving me with a barbecue beef sandwich to consume) and asked for one-half dozen more Lackey's tamales, announcing he'd finally found something spicy enough for his taste. The less-greasy tamale (Rhoda does use chicken fat, as you now know) that bore the Lackey name was packed with shredded chicken and a hell of a lot of spices, both Cajun and Mexican in flavor. Combined with masa, it had the flavor of a strong Frito chili pie.

Grav was just as enamored, if not more so, with the cheese dip. Touched, swallowed, gobbled, licked the bowl—these terms all apply to what Grav was doing to that sausage- and spice-packed bowl of cheese dip. When he ran out of chips he dolloped the dip onto his tamales. He sweated. The sweat rolled from the top of his head to the neck of his shirt, and he still could not get enough of it. He lauded it, calling it the best cheese dip he had ever tasted. He wiped his brow. He ate more. He inhaled those tamales and that cheese dip and would have rented an extra stomach if possible to be

Newport native Sonny Burgess became a big name for Sun Records out of Memphis. The lead singer for several bands, including the Rocky Road Ramblers and the Moonlighters, eventually settled down heading the Pacers. He's shared the stage with Elvis Presley, Carl Perkins, Charlie Rich, Jerry Lee Lewis and Conway Twitty, among others. Sonny Burgess and the Pacers were inducted into the Rockabilly Hall of Fame in 2002.

able to keep passing more of that spicy food through his lips. All of this amused me.

I had myself an order of fries and that jumbo barbecue beef sandwich topped with a dollop of coleslaw. It came with very little sauce, which I augmented with more from the table squeeze bottle, its flavor a cross between the thick sweet sauce of Old Post BBQ in Russellville and the tang of Sims Bar-B-Que's sauce from Little Rock. This barbecue juice was as thick as ketchup and on the orange side of brown, and it stuck to the meat with fervor.

I have never before encountered such a coarsely chopped brisket for a barbecue sandwich. This one had chunks of still-barked beef upon it, the rind edge of the brisket, one-half inch thick in places. That is not to say this made the quality poorer; in fact, I was thrilled to be able to sink my teeth into brisket that resembled what came from my own kitchen, thick with hickory smoke and a touch of rosemary. It was a sandwich that made you feel like you'd actually involved yourself in the eating of it rather than just letting something soft slide down your throat. The slaw was the perfect accompaniment, a little creamy with big chunks of white-ish cabbage laid in a circle under the bun.

So it was at eight o'clock on a Friday evening that we each found the perfect meal awaiting us at this comfortable brown-clad building alongside the main drag south of downtown Newport.

So what happened to Lackey's? Why did the restaurant disappear, and how did those tamales come to be on the Smokehouse BBQ menu? It all goes back to Clint Lackey. Now, Clint didn't actually come up with the recipe for the tamales—that recipe came from a street vendor in town eons ago—but he did produce them and the name stuck. It used to be that you could get them at Lackey's restaurant and through the factory at Tuckermann, which sent tamales out to be sold in stores hither and thither. The factory burned in 2012.

Along the way, Clint Lackey struck up a business with Scott Whitmire, and the two ran both the Lackey's restaurant and Smokehouse BBQ before

A pot full of Pasquale's Tamales in their "juice." *Grav Weldon*.

Most folks in Helena–West Helena know the Burger Shack by its motto, "Best Coke in Town." *Grav Weldon*.

Pulled pork and bottled sauce at Jones' Barbecue Diner, Marianna. *Grav Weldon.*

Below: A strawberry sundae at the Mammoth Orange Café in Redfield. *Kat Robinson*.

Right: Couch's Corner closed a few years ago, but two other family-run locations still endure in Paragould and Trumann. *Grav Weldon*.

Bottom: Presley's Drive In in Jonesboro makes one mean Reuben sandwich. *Kat Robinson*.

This thirty-three-ounce porterhouse steak with sides at Taylor's Steakhouse in Dumas was meant for two. *Grav Weldon*.

Sue's Kitchen in Jonesboro is a good place for not only burgers and fries but crab cakes as well. *Grav Weldon*.

Chicken gizzards are one of the many local favorites offered at Walker's Dairy Freeze in Marked Tree. *Gray Weldon.*

Shadden's Bar-B-Q in Marvell still appears ready to open, though its proprietor died years ago. *Gray Weldon.*

Left: Barbecue sandwiches, like this one at Kibb's Bar-B-Q #2 in Stuttgart, are usually offered with coleslaw under the bun. *Kat Robinson.*

Right: A hamburger at Bonnie's Café in Watson. *Kat Robinson.*

The catfish sandwich at Gene's Barbecue in Brinkley. *Kat Robinson.*

The Triangle Café in Batesville is popular with the local crowd who come for lunches and for breakfast favorites, like these pancakes. *Kat Robinson*.

The Roast Prime of Beef at Colonial Steakhouse in Pine Bluff is known for being a two-meal steak. *Kat Robinson*.

The Four Star Salad at Elizabeth's in Batesville includes tuna, shrimp, chicken and pasta salads with pickled okra. *Kat Robinson*.

The Front Page Café in Jonesboro. *Grav Weldon*.

This Double Hutt Burger at the Sno-White Grill in Pine Bluff is named for the Hutt Building Material Company a few blocks away. *Kat Robinson*.

Right: Deviled eggs are one of the options for salad at the Country Kitchen restaurant in Pine Bluff. *Kat Robinson*.

Below: Diners at the Parachute Inn in Walnut Ridge can consume their repast within the fuselage of a Southwest Airlines passenger jet. *Grav Weldon*.

The seasonally offered strawberry shortcake at the Bulldog Drive In in Bald Knob has become famous. Some individuals travel from out of state to enjoy the old-fashioned dessert. *Kat Robinson*.

The Chicken Special at Parkview Restaurant in Corning is an entire chicken dismembered, battered and deep fried, served with roasted potatoes. *Grav Weldon*.

Batten's Bakery in Paragould offers dozens of different pastries, such as these fried honeybuns. *Gran Weldon*.

Taco Rio's famed Taco Burger includes everything you get inside a taco on a hamburger bun. Cheese sauce or chili is extra and popular. *Gran Weldon*.

The distinctive flavor of the burgers and steaks offered at Jerry's Steakhouse in Trumann come from a custom-made flaming grill. *Gray Weldon*.

Chef Joe Cartwright's interpretation of a Delta classic: roasted herbed catfish, root vegetables and coleslaw. He works with fresh local meats and produce at the Wilson Café in Wilson. *Kat Robinson*.

Lasagna, made from old Marconi family recipes, at Uncle John's in Crawfordsville. *Kat Robinson*.

Like many Delta restaurants, Cotham's Mercantile in Scott offers daily lunch specials, such as the meatloaf seen here. *Kat Robinson*.

Coconut meringue pies, fresh out of the oven, cool on the counter at Charlotte's Eats and Sweets in Keo. *Kat Robinson.*

Pie is the default dessert served with barbecue around the Arkansas Delta, like this fried coconut pie with the smoked half chicken dinner at Demo's Smokehouse in Jonesboro. *Kat Robinson.*

Mexico Chiquito founder Blackie Donnelly created cheese dip in Arkansas in the 1940s. This example from Smokehouse BBQ in Newport contains Cajun spices and pulled pork. *Gray Weldon*.

Bread pudding is a popular dessert at sit-down restaurants in the Delta. This delectable version is the only dessert on the menu at Murry's Restaurant near Hazen. *Kat Robinson*.

Above: A crawfish boil is one of the many options offered on the buffet at Dondie's White River Princess in Des Arc. *Grav Weldon*.

Left: Fried green tomatoes, a southern classic, are a popular side dish. This marvelous example comes from Colby's Café and Catering in Wynne. *Kat Robinson*.

Homemade sauces, like the asiago cream sauce on this dish of chicken cannelloni, are part of the allure at Lazzari Italian Oven in Jonesboro. *Grav Weldon*.

getting to run both was too much. Clint ended up giving the business to Scott, and he's run it since. The old Lackey's is now a bar on the other side of town, and the Smokehouse keeps the tradition and recipes going. You can't get Lackey's in the grocery store, but you can still pick up frozen ones at Smokehouse to take home.

THE HUNGRY MAN RESTAURANT, NEWPORT

Out of the ashes of one great Arkansas restaurant chain came Newport's best burger joint. The chain in question was Wes Hall's indomitable Minute Man. From its roots in 1948, the Minute Man became the burger palace of choice for many Arkansas communities. The chain's innovations changed the face of what we know now as fast food, starting with the introduction of the Radar Range Pie, co-operative marketing giveaways like free Coca-Cola glasses with purchase, the Magic Meal (the first kids meal, two years before

The Hungry Man Restaurant in Newport. *Grav Weldon.*

McDonald's created the Happy Meal) and even a burger with special sauce (before the Big Mac).

But when the franchise died in the 1980s, some locations managed to keep going. Today there's just one Minute Man left (in El Dorado), and in Newport, the chain's heir is the Hungry Man. Started in 1977, by Carroll and Jeanette Wilson, it's still a charbroiling hub for northeast Arkansas.

The Wilsons already owned three grocery stores (one in Newport, two in nearby Tuckermann) when they bought into Minute Man. They thought it would be easy to run. It was anything but. Jeanette managed the restaurant and kept it going. They sold off the grocery stores in 2001.

Once the name was changed and the last vestiges of Minute Man were gone, the Wilsons turned the menu into their own, adding flame-broiled steaks and smoked meats to their repertoire. They even added a signature sandwich called the Three Little Pigs—smoked pork, smoked sausage and bacon on a bun. It's still one of the only places you can get a bona fide original Hickory Burger.

Of all things, the restaurant's become very well known for its cakes. Baked fresh daily, slices line the counter in clear plastic boxes—red velvet, peanut butter, chocolate, strawberry and Italian cream. If you drop by, you have to take some cake home with you.

Raw Apple Cake

Speaking of cakes, my friend Susan Harrington shares this recipe for a raw apple cake. "My grandmother's name was Inez Golden and was known to most of her grandchildren as Mama Golden," she told me. "She lived most of her life on a farm just outside of Greenway, Arkansas and was an amazing cook. She raised five children and had twelve grandchildren."

1 cup sugar
1 stick (½ cup) butter
1 egg
1½ cups all-purpose flour
1 teaspoon baking soda
1¼ teaspoon salt
1 teaspoon vanilla
½ cup black coffee, brewed
2 cups apples, peeled and chopped

Topping:
¼ cup sugar
½ cup coconut flakes
½ cup chopped walnuts or pecans

Note: Throughout the recipe, do as little mixing as possible, combing ingredients just until blended.

Heat oven to 350 degrees. Prepare a 9 x 13 cake pan. Beat together sugar and butter; add the egg. Mix together flour, salt and baking soda; slowly add to sugar mixture. Add vanilla and coffee and mix. Fold in the apples by hand. Mix together sugar, coconut flakes and chopped nuts and sprinkle on top. Bake for 30 minutes, checking after 20 to 25 minutes. Serves 8.

HOXIE

Up the road from Newport, the next spot of civilization is actually two cities. Hoxie and Walnut Ridge sit right next to each other and share a total population of about eight thousand people. But why aren't they just one town? It has to do with the railroad. Back in the 1870s, Walnut Ridge wanted the Kansas City, Springfield and Memphis Railroad to come through town, but no one could agree where the tracks should lay or the depot be built. The city itself couldn't purchase enough contiguous land to build a terminal. However, there was a lady who lived right south of town who was willing to make it happen. Mary Boas approached railroad officials and suggested that the railroad use her land, allowing it the right of way for no charge. Well, of course that was going to work. Boas and her husband, Henry, built a hotel near those tracks, and in 1888, Lawrence County accepted a petition to incorporate the town of Hoxie—which, incidentally, is named for railroad executive H.M. Hoxie of the St. Louis, Iron Mountain and Southern Railroad.

Hoxie is probably best known for school integration. In 1955, the Hoxie School District became the third in the state (after Fayetteville and Charleston) to integrate its school in compliance with the Supreme Court's landmark *Brown v. Board of Education of Topeka* ruling. It was going so smoothly that *Life* magazine sent a reporter to cover opening day on July 11, 1955, an unremarkably quiet day. However, after a photo essay about the event went to press, more than three hundred local segregationists poured into town to protest, announcing a boycott of schools by white students.

Ten days later, members of the Little Rock chapter of White America attended a segregation rally in Hoxie, at which a petition listing one thousand signatures was presented, demanding the resignation of the entire Hoxie school board. You read that right—the *Little Rock chapter* came to town to oust the Hoxie School Board. Well, of course those board members stayed right where they were, and then-governor Orval Faubus soon announced that the state wasn't going to intervene. Fed up with harassment from segregationists, the school board eventually filed suit against them. That suit was settled on October 25, 1956, when the Eighth Circuit Court of Appeals ruled in favor of the Hoxie School Board.

Most folks don't hear about the peaceful integration at Hoxie, though, because of the events of 1957 at Central High School in Little Rock.

THE PIZZA DEN

Hoxie is home to the Pizza Den, which first opened in 1989. Cliff Kinzer had worked for years in Baton Rouge, Louisiana, operating several restaurants and a wholesale supply warehouse. He and his wife retired young and moved to Ravenden, where the family raised cows. The restaurant bug was still with Cliff and the Pizza Den soon followed. Today, Cliff's daughters Tonya Stacy and Gobbie Milgrim, along with Gobbie's husband, Jonathan, keep the place running.

"We do make our own dough for the pizzas, po' boys and all the bread," Gobbie Milgrim told me. "We also slow cook our own roast and make our own chocolate chips cookies from scratch. Some of our more popular items

The Pizza Den in Hoxie. *Grav Weldon.*

are our pepper steak po' boys made from our slow-cooked roast and our cookie dough pizza made with our chocolate chip cookie dough."

But they make a lot more there, including fried chicken, catfish and pasta. The restaurant is also one of the very few places in the state where you'll find beignets on the menu.

Hoxie itself has fewer than three thousand residents, and for them, the Pizza Den is part of the community. Milgrim told me about a pregnant lady who went into labor but came by to get a pepper steak before heading into the hospital. And then there was the time the building next door caught fire: "A family had to drive their little girl by the restaurant at midnight to show her the Pizza Den hadn't burned down so she could get to sleep. She was so worried."

The Pizza Den's not going anywhere. You'll spot it alongside U.S. Highway 67 opposite the railroad tracks. It's hard to miss the prominent stone construction. "My sister and I have grown up with our customers. They are like family," Gobbie confirmed.

> Robert "Washboard Sam" Brown was born in Walnut Ridge in 1910. One of the early pioneers of the blues and purported half-brother of blues musician Big Bill Broonzy, he moved first to Memphis and then to Chicago, where he recorded more than 160 tracks. Unable to make the transition from acoustic to electric blues, he retired from music in 1949 and became a Chicago police officer. Brown died in 1966.

WALNUT RIDGE

Walnut Ridge was actually settled along the first low ridge of the Ozarks to the west of the current town in 1860. Word that the railroad was going to pass through the plain to the east got around, and a little more than ten years later most of the town had moved to its current location. Colonel Willis Miles Ponder, a Civil War veteran from Missouri, formally founded the town of Walnut Ridge in 1875 and became its first mayor. Incidentally, Walnut Ridge's move set it right atop an existing community called Pawpaw (named for all the pawpaw trees in the area). Today, the city of Walnut Ridge isn't even on a ridge, and now you know why.

The city may have lost the railroad, but it gained an airport. During World War II, an air force flying school was located north of town. Pilots were trained on BT-13s there. In 1944, the air force traded the facility to the Marine Corps. Once the war ended, it became a storage depot and dismantling base. At one point there were more than ten thousand planes held there, the largest number of aircraft ever amassed at one place. Williams Baptist College, which had started up in Pocahontas in 1941, moved into part of the facility in 1946. These are still not the biggest events that happened at that airport.

POLAR FREEZE, WALNUT RIDGE

Jack Allison has it made. Every day he wants to, he goes in to work at a restaurant he founded in 1958. He gets to sit down with his friends, who come by for coffee or a morning milkshake, and chew the fat with them. He smokes hams and makes burgers and when he wants to take off for a day or a week, he can do that.

Allison's place is the Polar Freeze in Walnut Ridge. Fifty-six years ago he started up the drive-in along U.S. Highway 67, and through the years his three kids and his wife have helped him out. The kids ended up going off to college and starting families of their own, and his wife eventually retired from the business three years ago. But Allison keeps on going.

The Polar Freeze is an institution around town. The oldest restaurant there, it still offers carhop service and a place to sit down and enjoy your meal indoors. Unlike other drive-in restaurants, there's far more than burgers and fries on the menu. There's also barbecued ham.

Jack Allison's Polar Freeze in Walnut Ridge. *Grav Weldon.*

"I barbecue fresh hams," Allison states, "that's all I've ever barbecued. Most people barbecue Boston butts or shoulders, maybe because they are cheaper, but they are a little greasier from my experience. I like fresh hams and I have a batch cooking right now that's going to come off in a couple, three hours."

I'd interrupted Allison twice this morning, first when he had been talking with a family and their little girl and again now, when his buddies were having their coffee fix. But he was affable and once I got him talking, he just kept on rolling:

> I bought it on the first of July 1958 and have been here on this corner all these years. I have a manager that's been with me about thirty-five years, an assistant manager twenty-five years, and when I really want to do something I just plan it and go do it!
>
> Walnut Ridge is a little old town. We have about four thousand population here, and everybody's been real good to me. I've had pretty good business all these years. I couldn't have had a better life. I just enjoy it mainly because I get to see all my friends. They're good friends, but they're not going to knock on your front door when you're retired. They will come by and get coffee or a milk shake and talk. If I have a day off with nothing to do I'm just bored.

I had to ask him about the crazy day that the town has recently received a lot of notice for. On September 18, 1964, a particular musical group had a stopover in the town and Jack Allison is the man credited with the discovery. He laughed when I asked.

> They give me credit for it, but I really don't deserve the credit. I was picking up paper and trash off the lot at maybe ten, eleven o'clock at night and I saw this large plane circling. We have a wonderful airport at Walnut Ridge—I thought it was unusual to see it come through the night. About that time, three teenagers came running around in a car. I asked them what they were doing and they said "trying to run around" so I told them to go check on the airport and see what was going on with that plane, and here they went.
>
> An hour later they came back all excited. They said it was the Beatles. Now, I said, "Don't come back into town starting some sort of rumor like that." "No, Jack, that's the Beatles," they said. I didn't believe it. Because I was stationed in England for thirty months and I was twenty miles from

Liverpool and that's where the Beatles started. And it was a coincidence, it really was the Beatles—so that's the story there. What I did, I did completely just to give those kids something to do.

At the time of this writing, Allison was eighty years old. Before we ended our conversation, I told him to have a good day. "At eighty years old, every day's a good day," he chuckled.

THE BEATLES AT WALNUT RIDGE

The Beatles had indeed come through that night, to change planes and head on for a day's rest at Reed Pigman's ranch up in Alton, Missouri. Word spread quickly about their visit, and on the rumor of a return through the airport, nearly three hundred people skipped church that Sunday morning and were on hand when the plane returned September 20. People took photos with the plane waiting to transport the famed musicians to their next destination. Family movies were shot, and teenagers sang Beatles songs. Sure enough, a plane carrying John Lennon and Ringo Starr landed that morning.

At the Walnut Ridge depot, you'll find the Guitar Walk. The 115-foot-long by 40-foot-wide concrete depiction of an Epiphone guitar is accompanied by interpretive panels celebrating the great musicians of Rock 'N' Roll Highway 67, including Johnny Cash, Jerry Lee Lewis, Carl Perkins, Roy Orbison, Conway Twitty, Sonny Burgess, Billy Lee Riley, Wanda Jackson and Elvis Presley.

What the crowd didn't know was that Paul McCartney and George Harrison had already come to Walnut Ridge in an old pickup truck. They joined their colleagues, walked a gauntlet of thrilled fans and boarded the plane. The whole incident didn't take long, but it left a permanent memory on the town.

Today, you can walk Abbey Road in Walnut Ridge. There, you'll find a yellow submarine. Businesses all over town embrace the Beatles tie. In 2010, an artist by the name of Danny White created a sculpture that's become a landmark: silhouettes of the Fab Four against a shiny sculpted wall. Yes, you can have your photo taken with the silhouettes

Beatles Park in Walnut Ridge. *Grav Weldon.*

of the Beatles, and each September, the city commemorates that little stopover with the Beatles at the Ridge Music Festival. Learn more at beatlesattheridge.com.

THE PARACHUTE INN, WALNUT RIDGE

The Walnut Ridge Regional Airport is worth a visit, not just for its Beatles connection or for the neat air museum that commemorates its role in World War II or the planes that came to the facility afterward, but for its restaurant.

At that very same airfield where the Beatles came through in 1964 sits a strange little eatery. Strange, that is, not for the food but for the fact that its main dining room is the fuselage of a Boeing 737 passenger jet. The place is the Parachute Inn.

The restaurant's new fuselage has just been added to an older restaurant that served the community since 1968. Harold and Janie Johnson ran the little diner next to the airstrip over all those years. But in 2004, new owner Donna Roberts bought the majority of an old Southwest Airlines jet and started the conversion, which included laying the plane on its belly and building

Inside the Parachute Inn's dining room, the fuselage of a Southwest Airlines passenger jet. Note the signatures on the overhead compartments. *Grav Weldon.*

a connecting staircase and hangar. Rhonda Higginbotham purchased the property in 2008.

Today, you have a choice when you go in—settling for sitting close to the buffet line inside the original restaurant building, or going up the steps and choosing a spot along the ninety-two-foot open area of the plane. Kids often take over the cockpit, which is full of dials and levers and overhead details like you'd find in any jet. Some of the main body's seats have been removed for tables; other seats have been reversed to face the same way, just like a booth in a restaurant. Overhead, the old luggage compartments bear the signatures of hundreds of Southwest Airline employees who have made the journey to Walnut Ridge just to dine in the old aircraft.

The gimmick of dining in the jet isn't the only draw. The restaurant has become well known for serving up spicy catfish, chicken livers and other local classics alongside burgers and fries. Dessert is always homemade, and the chocolate cake must come from the same recipe my ancestors utilized, complete with chocolate icing—not frosting—on top.

Pocahontas and Corning

U.S. Highway 67 shoots due north from Walnut Ridge to collide with the edge of the Ozarks in Pocahontas. The oldest soda fountain in the state,

Futrell Pharmacy, is located on that ridge downtown—on the edge of the Arkansas Ozarks (its story is included in *Classic Eateries of the Ozarks and Arkansas River Valley*). Indeed, the Delta arguably begins just two blocks away, on the banks of the Black River.

Pocahontas is one of the oldest towns in Arkansas. The first post office founded in the state back in 1817 was in Davidsonville, a few miles to the west. Originally called Bettis' Bluff, Pocahontas was incorporated and received its permanent name in 1835. It serves as the Randolph County seat and retains its 1872 Italianate courthouse. Randolph County is the only county in Arkansas crossed by five different rivers.

U.S. Highway 67 darts east to Corning. This little town close to the state's northern border used to be a popular stop for travelers. Originally named Hecht City and centered around Levi and Solomon Hecht's lumber mill on the Black River, the town moved west to take advantage of the new Cairo and Fulton Railroad that ran through Clay County. It was named for H.D. Corning, a rail engineer, in 1873. Apparently the way to have a city named after you in the nineteenth century was to work for a railroad!

PARKVIEW RESTAURANT, CORNING

Corning is one of two county seats for Clay County (the other being Piggott to the east). It benefits from being the first town with any sort of facilities on the south side of the Missouri border. For many years, several hotels operated there for travelers coming into the state. Of them, the Parkview has kept a strong clientele through the years. Originally the Parkview Tourist Court and later Rusty's Parkview Motel and Restaurant, the facility is commemorated in a series of postcards issued over the decades. One reads:

> *Offering all conveniences to the traveling public. Twenty-eight rooms, tile baths, air-conditioning, telephone in every room, controlled heat, free television, Simmons Beauty Rest mattresses, free swimming pool. Beautiful city park adjoining for your pleasure. Restaurant and auto services next to motel. A really delightful place to stop.*

Today, the Parkview Restaurant serves as community center for generations of town residents. Barely changed from the 1950s, it serves steaks, catfish and

East of Corning on U.S. Highway 62, you'll come to the town of Piggott, about as far northeast as you can get in the state. While the village's classic eateries have all disappeared, it's worth a visit to the Arkansas home of Ernest Hemingway. The famed author lived with wife Pauline Pfeiffer in her parent's home for a few years. Today, you can tour the home and visit the barn loft where Hemingway wrote most of *A Farewell to Arms*. Learn more about Hemingway's Arkansas years in Dr. Ruth Hawkins's book, *Unbelievable Happiness and Final Sorrow*.

fried chicken. Its ancient tables and booths offer a respite from travel and a good, hearty meal.

There's a special you should consider when you're dining there. The Chicken Special is $10.99 and includes a whole fried chicken. No, not all together—it's actually cut into pieces, battered and fried while you wait. It takes about twenty-five minutes from the moment you order to when it arrives at the table, and it comes with grill-roasted potato halves. And it's worth every nickel and every minute and every bite.

Like most good Delta restaurants, it has pie—in this case a coconut cream pie that's just divine, made from scratch from the crust up.

7

THE LONG ROADS

U.S. Highway 49, Arkansas Highway 1 and Crowley's Ridge Parkway

U.S. HIGHWAY 49

U.S. Highway 49 gets its fame from that incident where bluesman Robert Johnson allegedly sold his soul to the Devil at its intersection with U.S. Highway 61 in Mississippi. In Arkansas, it cuts a crescent through the Delta, entering at Helena–West Helena and curling west and then northeast to bisect Brinkley and Jonesboro before reaching its northern terminus at Piggott.

Unlike most of the other federal highways through Arkansas that were formed when the system first came online in 1926, most of U.S. Highway 49 through Arkansas wasn't built until the 1960s. It was first extended from Clarksville, Mississippi, to Brinkley in 1963 (replacing Arkansas Highway 6), farther north to Jonesboro in 1978 (replacing Arkansas Highway 39) and finally to Piggott via concurrency with Arkansas Highway 1. From Brinkley north, it runs parallel to the St. Louis Southwestern rail line, better known as the Cotton Belt Route.

Crowley's Ridge Parkway came later. It was first designated an Arkansas Scenic Byway in 1997 before becoming a National Scenic Byway in 2000 with the addition of a fourteen-mile stretch in Missouri. At its southern end, it runs concurrent with U.S. Highway 49 before splitting north of Helena–West Helena to crawl on a narrow two-lane road through the Saint Francis National Forest up to Marianna. There, it splits off the Great River Road and heads north along Arkansas Highway 1. The designation skips back and forth between highway and county roads, always running alongside or atop

Crowley's Ridge, passing through cities and the largest Arkansas state park, Village Creek State Park.

Crowley's Ridge itself is a geological oddity. Situated in the middle of the Mississippi River Alluvial Plain in Arkansas, it rises from 200 to 550 feet in elevation along the Mississippi Embayment for around 150 miles, mostly in Arkansas. Benjamin Crowley gave it his name. He was the first settler known to have built a home there, back in 1820. It's made of loess (pronounced "luss")—mostly windborne sediment, quite different from the black, rich soil of the Delta.

Communities dot the two lines across the central and northern sections of the Arkansas Delta. Among them are some of the Delta's more definitive restaurants.

PENNY'S PLACE, WEINER

In the summer of 1996, I discovered Lake Hogue. I left work at nine o'clock each morning and found it impossible to sleep during the day, so in summer I would go fishing, sometimes by myself, sometimes with my boyfriend. It wasn't far from Jonesboro and sitting on the dam or slinging a line into the lake or Bayou De View right next to it was sure to net some catfish, crappie or sunfish (and one night, a very irritated and large gar).

When we tired of making the attempt, a stop at J&D's Dairy Bar in Weiner was in order. Jackie and Darrel Bryant—the J and D in the name—built the

Penny's Place in Weiner. *Grav Weldon.*

little dairy bar across from a rice gin in 1972. Jackie would invariably be around, and the burgers and dipped cones were always perfect after a sweaty, stinky morning of fishing. She never complained about our appearance, despite the fact that she kept the place neat as a pin.

The Bryants ran the place until 2004, when it was purchased by Penny Sitzer. Very little has changed, besides the name and a few additions to the menu. I made my first return visit back to the little dairy bar in the summer of 2010 while working on a breakfast cover story for the *Arkansas Times*. I left Little Rock at four o'clock in the morning, and at six o'clock, I arrived to find the place packed with locals. I found a single spot to perch and immediately had Sitzer's attention. She brought me a coffee cup before I could even ask and gave me every bit of attention everyone else in the duck blind-inspired interior was getting. The coffee was hot, and Sitzer managed to steal my heart with homemade biscuits and cream gravy.

"I bought it because I just love to cook and feed people a good home cooked meal," Sitzer shared with me in a Facebook message. "This year I've added a barbecue shed to cook ribs, butts and burgers all off the grill."

You could smell it, too, when we went by on our research trip in March 2013. While breakfast was being served, the scent of rubbed butts smoking in the shed drew more people in off U.S. Highway 49, almost like magic. She's also added frog legs, hand-battered chicken-fried steaks and barbecue burgers, which she sauces and smokes, that taste just like what you'd get at a backyard get-together. Sitzer's also taken to making cinnamon rolls. Every bit of the new menu seems to be winning more return customers.

Josie's is a famed steakhouse—we'll get into its history on page 188. Attached under the same roof, you'll find the Dairy Shack, or D-Shack, which has been around since rocks were soft. D-Shack's burgers are flat and juicy, and you have to tell the cook what you want on them, since there's no default choice for condiments or such. There's a daily lunch special for $4.99, a meat-and-two-veg special that features things like a chopped steak, fried chicken or chopped pork barbecue, locally farm raised catfish, tilapia and shrimp. Barbecue sandwiches start at $1.90, and there are nine different flavors of milkshake—including peanut butter, pineapple, butterscotch and cherry. *Grav Weldon.*

If you are lucky, and I mean very lucky, you might chance on Penny's Place when the chocolate rolls are just coming out. Similar to cinnamon rolls, these cocoa-infused swirls are legendary.

WOODY'S BAR-B-Q, WALDENBURG

William Wood never intended to get into the barbecue business. He was a cropduster pilot and spent many seasons over the fields of the north Delta. Starting in 1985, during the spring and fall, Woody and his wife, Cecelia, set up their RV at the four-way stop where U.S. Highway 49 meets Arkansas Highway 14, selling barbecue to passersby to earn a little money they could go fishing on.

Thing is, Woody had himself some good barbecue, and it got popular.

"We never actually intended on doing what we done," he told me. "We got to coming over to this four-way stop in Waldenburg, and we had a motor home and we'd sit at the four-way stop, selling barbecue for fun. It finally got out of hand and got big enough in 1992, I finally just had to crawl out of the airplane and do barbecue full time."

Woody and Cecelia's operation took off. Today, the scent of roasting meat could pull you right off the highway. No beef here—Woody only smokes pork and chicken.

The smoke's good, but it's the sauce that made Woody's famous. "We started doing a lot of catering, and we came up with this barbecue sauce," he continued. "Everybody kept wanting to buy it. We would make it in our carport on a fish cooker in a three-gallon pot.

"One day, someone came by and asked for just a cup of sauce and we sold it to him. We figured if people would buy just the sauce, we needed to sell that sauce. Took us two years to sell that first bottle. We sold that first bottle in 1996, and we come up with the dry rub barbecue seasoning in 1999. Now we're shipping it all over the country. We built a four-thousand-square-foot facility where we make and package our own products, and we pack for other people."

I asked him if he'd go back to cropdusting if he could.

"Not really, no. The rules and regulations have gotten to be so much. I miss the old airplanes a little bit but the other part of it, no, I wouldn't want to get back in there."

Twenty years of cropdusting and another thirty years of barbecue have made it a long stretch for Woody and Cecelia. They're hoping someone might eventually come through and buy out the operation and keep on making Woody's Bar-B-Q sauce and seasoning. Their three children all have jobs of their own and no interest in taking it on. For now, they're still hanging out at the four-way stop whenever the weather's right every Wednesday, Thursday and Friday night.

Here's a secret: you can make a killer barbecue party dip out of Woody's dry rub. The recipe:

Woody's Bar-B-Q Dip

8 ounces sour cream
2 tablespoons Miracle Whip salad dressing
2 tablespoons Woody's Dry Rub

Blend all ingredients together and refrigerate. Stays good up to three weeks, but it usually won't last that long. Serve with crackers or chips.

WYNNE

The city of Wynne began in 1882 when a train on the St. Louis, Iron Mountain and Southern Railroad derailed. One of the boxcars was uprighted and named Wynne Station in honor of Captain Jesse Wynne of Forrest City, who, surprisingly enough from this book's perspective, was not a railroad worker or magnate but a banker who had established the Bank of Eastern Arkansas.

More rails and trains were to come, and in 1885 the burg became the hub for construction of a line that would run from Memphis to Bald Knob (a route now traced by

Peebles Farm, located between McCrory and Augusta on U.S. Highway 64, has become famous for its annual corn maze. Each year, the folks that run this pick-your-own farm come up with a new design for the maze, which often includes designs that can be spotted from overhead. Previous year's designs include tractors, a riverboat, a barn, a duck, a spider's web and even the county courthouse. It also offers pick-your-own cotton. Learn more at peeblesfarm.com.

U.S. Highway 64). Full of rail workers, Wynne became a true Western town with five saloons, two hotels, a blacksmith, grocery and general stores and all the trappings of a pop-up city for folks who had money in pocket—and that was just in two years! Then, a fire on September 2, 1887, burned a lot of the new businesses.

Wynne didn't quit. Almost everything was rebuilt. The next year Lon D. Freeman established the Wynne *Ripsaw*, which would be renamed the *Wynne Progress* in 1904. The east–west line started operation in 1888, and the town was incorporated. To this day, no one knows why it was named for Captain Wynne, but the name stuck. In 1907, a bottling plant opened there, eventually producing Nehi and Royal Crown Cola in 1940.

There's no doubting that a town created by folks who worked on the railroad was made up of real characters. Back in the 1930s, H.K. Barwick owned the town's automotive dealership. His brother, Chip, owned a similar operation in Memphis. H.K. reportedly had his brother and some other folks out duck hunting and came up with a crazy idea—take their live decoys (yes, live ducks, which were legal back then) and place them in the fountain inside the most regal hotel in all of Memphis. Which they then did. Today, you can watch the Peabody Ducks in their fountain in the lobby of the Peabody Hotel, though, these ducks are definitely not decoys.

KELLEY'S RESTAURANT, WYNNE

U.S. Highway 64's path includes a large section of the Trail of Tears. It roughly parallels U.S. Highway 70 to the north. A corridor between the roads is home to Interstate 40 and to a portion of the Big Woods, which includes wetlands of the Cache, White and Arkansas River and Bayou De View.

Coming into Wynne heading east on U.S. Highway 64, you'll encounter a large restaurant that's been around since the 1950s, the last remnant of a dining giant that once spread throughout northeast Arkansas. The restaurant traces its lineage back to the proprietor of a little "cracker box" called the Night Hawk in Batesville. Jeff Kelley was good at running the restaurant and opened more—some around Batesville and some in other cities, including Newport, Pocahontas, Bald Knob and Wynne. He set up each of his four kids with those out-of-city restaurants, and they all thrived.

Batesville's Kelley-Wyatt's Restaurant and Bald Knob's Kelley's Restaurant managed to stay in business until 2013, but the other locations all withered away earlier, with the exception of the lone restaurant in Wynne. That's a shame, since Jeff Kelley's smorgasbord was one of the first buffets in the state.

In Wynne, Kelley's is run by Jeff's grandson, Shannon Kelley. It offers a seafood buffet on Friday nights and banquet-style meals any time. There's always pie in the case, and chances are, if you go on a Saturday, you'll probably notice someone's wedding party come through.

JOHNSON'S FREEZE INN & FISH HOUSE, WYNNE

At U.S. Highway 64 and Arkansas Highway 1 in Wynne, there's a flat sprawl of a restaurant that's a little bit of everything. It appears to be a big restaurant on one side, a small dairy drive-thru on the other, and its lineage is all over the place. This is Johnson's, though whether you want to call it Johnson's Freeze Inn or Johnson's Fish House or Johnson's Diner is up to you. It's both one restaurant and two, and there's even, at one time, been a third. Confused yet?

Back in 1970, it was Chuck's Bar-B-Q, and Carolyn Johnson went to work there. When the folks that were running it wanted to get out of the business,

Johnson's Freeze Inn & Fish House still has two phone numbers—one for hamburgers and one for the diner. *Grav Weldon.*

they offered it to Carolyn and her husband, W.C. Johnson. The deal stuck, and Chuck's became Big Johnson's. For thirty-five years, it was a marvelously fine place to get pork butt barbecue.

But in 2008, fire burned the restaurant. Carolyn Johnson was severely injured. While she recuperated, her daughter kept the business going in a food truck they dubbed Little Johnson's.

The restaurant was rebuilt, and it's now Johnson's Fish House, at least on one side. On the other side, it's Johnson's Freeze Inn, a dairy drive-in where you can get burgers. The restaurant also serves catfish and old family barbecue, too. It's one restaurant that's part diner, part drive-in and all pretty good eats.

ARKANSAS HIGHWAY 1

Johnson's isn't the only place to pick up a burger. Six blocks away, you'll find Skipper's Catfish and Hamburger Delight. It's in a little low-slung red building along the side of Arkansas Highway 1. The burgers are pretty decent, and the catfish is pretty satisfying.

The best burgers, in my opinion, come from Colby's Café and Catering. The large restaurant on the flat plain south of town does a little bit of everything—pasta, southern food and sandwiches. Colby's staff makes their own bread and some of the most amazing fried green tomatoes you can find anywhere.

Catty-corner across the street from Johnson's stands Hickory House BBQ. Located in an old dairy diner, Rick James's restaurant puts out

Skipper's Catfish and Hamburger Delight in Wynne. *Grav Weldon.*

simple barbecue low on the grease and high on the coleslaw. It's been open since 1991.

Heading south toward Forrest City, you'll eventually get to Mike's Family Restaurant. You'll know it from its green roof and the rocking chairs out front. Mike Linam originally planned, way back in 1993, to just have a store along Arkansas Highway 1. His little grocery store had a snackbar in it with hot things to eat. He worked with his wife and daughter and learned quickly how popular the snackbar was. It progressed over the years, and it wasn't long before he closed half the grocery store and expanded the snackbar into a restaurant. Eventually the restaurant took over the whole place.

Mike's is known for great steaks and catfish (all United States pond raised), for sandwiches and for great desserts—including top-to-bottom homemade pies in chocolate, coconut, pecan, apple, cherry, lemon icebox, strawberry and whatever else is requested.

Then there's Catfish Island. Opened in 1988, it's the go-to place for regional catfish lovers. Catfish Island is all about the catfish, hush puppies and slaw. There's a salad bar and desserts, but catfish is the be-all and end-all of reasons to cross over to the Caldwell community for a bite.

HARRISBURG

North of Wynne on Arkansas Highway 1, about halfway to Jonesboro, you'll find the community of Harrisburg. The town has seen a significant influx of new residents as Jonesboro has expanded, with many choosing to live in the smaller city.

The original go-to restaurant in town was Betty's Steak and Chicken, but Betty's closed its doors in early 2014.

Mel's Steakhouse, which stands a block off Arkansas Highway 1, still puts together some of the greatest,

Parker Pioneer Homestead is a re-created nineteenth-century town located six miles south of Harrisburg on a working farm. Every October, the homestead is opened up for a fall festival. It's home to a prize herd of Beltie cattle and has become renowned for its sorghum molasses and homemade fudge. Learn more at parkerhomestead.com.

meanest steak you can imagine. It was opened in 1977 by Melvin Redd, who used to cook at different times for the Arkansas Razorback football staff

Mel's Steakhouse is only open to patrons on Friday nights, though catering is available at other times. *Grav Weldon.*

and then-governor Bill Clinton. Most of Mel's business came from catering, and if there were any big events or outdoor fundraisers around Poinsett or Craighead Counties, you could follow your nose to wherever the grills were set up.

Melvin passed away in 2013, but the restaurant continues. It's only open to the public on Friday nights, and it's not very big. You enter through the kitchen and head to the back, where there are a few tables. The service isn't fancy, but the steaks are excellent.

8

THE METROPOLITAN DELTA

JONESBORO, PARAGOULD AND POINTS BEYOND

Jonesboro feels like a town out of its natural habitat. It doesn't feel like what the rest of the state feels like. That was one of the first thoughts I had about the place when I moved there in 1995. Over the three years I roamed the town and its surroundings, I never quite lost that feeling.

The town is one of two county seats in Craighead County—a county, I have to tell you, that was named out of spite. In 1858, Senator William Jones proposed carving the county out of land represented by fellow state senator Thomas Craighead, who thought the idea was asinine. The bill passed anyway, and when it did, Jones proposed that it be named for Craighead, who in turn proposed that the county seat be named for Jones. The town of "Jonesborough" was created. The name was simplified to Jonesboro before its official incorporation one-quarter century later.

The city flourished at the end of the nineteenth century thanks to timber rail lines, most notably with operators like Missouri Pacific, Frisco and Burlington Northern Santa Fe serving the area. The establishment of City Water and Light (CWL) in 1906 helped the city flourish, and even today, CWL keeps rates in town remarkably low. In 1910, the First District Agricultural School offered its first courses; this facility would eventually become Arkansas State University.

Jonesboro was home to the first woman to serve in the United States Senate, Hattie Caraway, who succeeded her husband after his death in 1932. It's also home to Olympic pole-vaulter Earl Bell and Miss America Debbye Turner and was the birthplace of noted novelist John Grisham.

In my mind, Jonesboro isn't a typical Arkansas town. The largest city on the east side of the state is the home of a burgeoning student population that brings new ideals to the area with each incoming class. It's a manufacturing and food production hub for gigantic operations such as Post and Frito Lay. It's a medical magnet with a couple huge hospitals treating what ails citizens of the Delta, and it's an agricultural crossroads that takes in the bounty of farmed produce and grain and returns it in packaged goods.

If Jonesboro was a person, it'd be a guy in a blue button-down shirt and overalls.

In the latter half of the 1990s, it was packed full of homegrown restaurants of every variety, including a heavy smattering of Asian offerings. Gee Street on the west side of town was home to a collection of cheap diners, drive-ins and ice cream joints. South Caraway had all the sit-down places. North Caraway catered to the college crowd, and way out in Nettleton there were great catfish and barbecue joints. There was always something neat and new to try in the town.

The old roots were strong. No one could remember quite how long Wyatt's Cafeteria had been in Indian Mall, or if there was a thrown-roll place before the Front Page Café. Places like Jason's Dairy Breeze and Frank's Eskimo Queen were frequented just the way they had been done a generation past, and the Galley still served big fat hush puppies.

When I started writing this book series, I was thrilled to be sharing more about this strange metropolitan place in the Delta. I had a score of restaurants to share, including five very old Chinese restaurants that I thought might seed more research on restaurants of that ilk through the Delta. I was heartened by a possible connection between these places and the Chinese-owned grocery stores researched in both Arkansas and Mississippi by the folks over at the Southern Foodways Alliance. Imagine my shock when I arrived in Jonesboro for a weekend of research in March of 2014 and found that every one of them was gone—every single one.

But it wasn't just the Asian restaurants. Jason's, Frank's, even the old standard of Couch's Corner Barbecue had met their end, mostly in the three years preceding my visit. In their place was a score of new enterprises. Mind you, some of them (especially the ones now crowding Jonesboro's Main Street downtown) are very welcome; Godsey's Grill, Skinny J's,

Omar's Uptown and Cregeen's Irish Pub are all locally owned mid-range restaurants that have given downtown the revival it so desperately needed. But the big chains came in with the loosening of liquor laws that allowed "private members" to purchase drinks with dinner, and places like Red Lobster, Applebee's, Buffalo Wild Wings and Olive Garden quickly choked out the homegrown restaurants.

It's stunning, what has happened. The town has long been known for having fantastic cheap eats, but they've evaporated. The price point has gone up, and the little operations have struggled. In the end, just a handful of the local restaurants have hung on to become classics.

There is irony in the fact that the big chains aren't doing so well in Jonesboro. There's another comparison to be made, too, just up the road in Paragould—a city half the size but better equipped to support its classics. In this city, you'll find the second-oldest bakery in the Delta, along with a holdout from the long-gone Dog n Suds chain and one of the most stunning gutbomb burgers you may ever encounter. Paragould keeps the Couch's name alive with its Couch's Bar-B-Q, run by another offshoot of the famed barbecue family.

The story of metropolitan classic dining in the Delta is truly a tale of two cities.

Jonesboro at one time was home to many Chinese restaurants. In 1996, those restaurants included Beijing Chinese Restaurant, Dragon City, Dragon & Phoenix, Great Wall of China, Hunan China, China Garden, Imperial Chinese, Kowloon and China Kitchen. Dragon and Phoenix was the last of Jonesboro's classic Chinese restaurants to close. *Grav Weldon.*

PARAGOULD

Paragould was built around rails and lumber. In 1872, the St. Louis and Iron Mountain Railroad began service through Arkansas between St. Louis, Missouri, and Texarkana. James W. Paramore, president of the Cotton Belt Railroad, wanted a way to ship Texas cotton to St. Louis and points beyond. In 1877, he made a deal to connect his Texas railroad line with the Iron Mountain in Texarkana. About that time, the Palmer and Sullivan railroad system was being developed in Mexico. Paramore's directors voted to expand their Texas railroad line to join the Mexican railway, giving St. Louis a direct connection through Arkansas and Texas to Mexico City.

Jay Gould, who gained control of the Iron Mountain Railroad in 1880, learned that Paramore's Texas—St. Louis Railroad was licensed to build a cheaper narrow-gauge line through Arkansas to Texas. Gould constructed a regular-gauge line to parallel Paramore's route that ran through Greene County toward Helena. Where they crossed, a community called Parmley popped up. However, postmaster Marcus Meriweather decided to name the town on his own volition—Para for Paramore and Gould for Gould. Thus in 1883, Paragould was born.

Weird things happening are a part of Paragould's history. In 1930, a meteorite streaked across the sky and came down four miles away in the Finch community; it weighed all of seventy-five pounds. In 1936, Frank Reynolds and Lloyd Rogers discovered large bones in a creek that turned out to be a ten-thousand-year-old mastodon.

BATTEN'S BAKERY, PARAGOULD

Batten's Bakery may have one of the strangest lineages of any Delta restaurant I know. See, Mike Batten is a Batten who owns Batten's Bakery in Paragould, but he may not be the Batten you are looking for. In fact, though Batten's Bakery has been around since 1954, I don't believe Mike has been around that long. And besides, Albert Batten wouldn't have had a clue who he was.

That doesn't change the power of the name of the oldest bakery in northeast Arkansas, nor does it invalidate the family's connection to pastry-making. Confused? Let me enlighten you.

Albert Batten started making doughnuts in a garage at Thompson and South Fifth Streets. It wasn't much of an operation at first, but it became a community staple. Batten would get up early in the morning and make doughnuts and sell them until they were gone. Customers say he didn't believe in day-olds, so if a regular came into the kitchen garage late in the day, he was apt to throw a few extra in to make sure they got gone. They were a bargain, too, at fifty cents a dozen. Over the years, the offerings expanded to cakes, pastries and such. A few individuals even claim that Elvis Presley was once spotted there downing a bearclaw—though the veracity of such a statement is doubtable.

Mike Batten is the latest Batten to run Batten's Bakery in Paragould. *Grav Weldon.*

Eventually the little garage kitchen became too small for the operation, so in 1965 Batten moved out and east one-half mile on Kingshighway to a spot that sat catty-corner to Dog n Suds (still in operation today). While still small, a few people could come in and have breakfast in the little eatery. Batten also made doughnuts for local grocery stores to sell, and his golden rings became the standard for the area.

Batten kept the bakery going for decades, but when his health waned, he was ready to pass it on. In 1980, he sold it to Bonnie Abbott, who had worked there since she was a young woman and who reportedly never worked at another establishment. In the 2000s, Leon Johnson bought the place and ran it for four years, through one of the worst financial times for bakeries anywhere, with the rise in prices of eggs, milk and flour.

Enter Mike and Bridgette Batten. The couple worked in the corporate world—he was a design engineer, she was a director of systems management—but while in the area in 2004 they happened to learn that the bakery was available. It seemed like providence, so soon the younger Battens had themselves a bakery. They've managed to collect many of the recipes used by both Albert Batten and by Bonnie Abbott, and they turn out a goodly number of baked goods six days a week for the citizens of Paragould.

As I mentioned in *Arkansas Pie: A Delicious Slice of the Natural State*, Batten's Bakery offers a rare traditional pie that is available nowhere else—a chocolate old-fashioned that's filled with cocoa, butter and sugar, not custard and certainly not pudding. The flavor of this pie, its flaky consistency and its density all remind me of the good things about growing up in Arkansas. It's certainly a pie a grandmother would have conjured.

Dog n Suds, Paragould

Dog n Suds isn't an Arkansas original by any means. The original restaurant was opened in Champaign, Illinois, in 1953 by Don Hamacher and Jim Griggs, two music teachers who just wanted to offer a place for kids to get hot dogs and root beer. The first Dog n Suds was so popular that a wealthy dowager paid them to build her another one, and soon Don and Jim were done with teaching music for a living and hot on the path of creating a franchise. Locations quickly spread, first throughout Illinois and Indiana and then into Ohio, Michigan and the rest of the United States. By 1970, there were six hundred Dog n Suds in thirty-eight states and Canada, and the eatery's popular creamy root beer had become well-known and well-liked.

In the 1970s, Dog n Suds merged with another restaurant chain, and the management at that chain eliminated the original formula root beer and replaced it. Original location owners started to break away, while others closed. The final insult came when the East Coast company that had taken on Dog n Suds sold the rights to the root beer recipe to a bottler in Michigan.

Those few locations that kept the original root beer and look of the drive-in manage to not only stay afloat but also to thrive. Many have incorporated under a new set of owners, Don and Carol VanDame, who purchased the rights and trademark in 1991. Their new company, TK&C's LLC, incorporated in 2001, has licensed the Dog n Suds brand.

Today, there are fourteen Dog n Suds locations left, the southernmost of which is in Paragould. It's one of the few locations with the original sign plus the ice cream cone—absent on most of the rest (see it on the front cover of this book). A mug of frosty, creamy root beer is $1.30, while you can take home a gallon for $4.50. Chili dogs and footlong hot dogs are still popular, but the menu has been expanded to include hamburgers, chicken strips, salads and even burritos. It's open six days a week, and from time to time you'll find someone who's made the pilgrimage to sit in their car and revel in this remaining slice of nostalgia.

PARAGOULD'S CLASSICS

Paragould residents have been able to get a Mexican restaurant fix for cheap since 1975, thanks to Taco Rio. It looks like it might be a chain operation, but it's actually a locally owned and operated Tex-Mex joint with very cheap prices. Tacos, burritos, enchiladas and nachos—this is the place in town to get your fix.

Orders coming out at Taco Rio in Paragould. *Grav Weldon.*

The Bar-B-Q Barn in Paragould is known both for great ribs and crispy catfish fillets. *Grav Weldon.*

Taco Rio is best known not for a taco but for a burger—one made from taco meat. In fact, the only difference between the taco burger and a taco is the bun in place of the shell. They're pretty good, but the real delight is having one covered in either chili or cheese dip.

The town is full of great places for cheap eats. Terry's Café downtown is one of those excellent little breakfast-and-lunch diners that always has whatever home cooking item you're really craving. BBQ Barn on the west side of town has marvelous barbecue and smoked chicken and some of the most notable catfish in town.

And then there's Hamburger Station. Situated in an old tile-topped Texaco station alongside the railroad tracks north of downtown (seen on this book's cover); the little eatery has a big following. The star of the show is the Humburger—an old-fashioned, fat sashy served with onions and mustard on a toasted bun. These little gutbombs have become notorious, adored by blue-collar workers and motorcyclists alike.

BARBECUE IN THE METROPOLITAN DELTA

I mentioned Couch's Bar-B-Que at the start of this chapter. During my KAIT days, Couch's was famous. It was *the* barbecue around town. Heading out to the east side of town for ribs was a thing back then.

Couch's Corner Bar-B-Q in Jonesboro had a good run, more than forty years of great smoked meats dating back to 1970. It went under a few years ago, but the family continues the tradition at two other locations. Couch's Bar-B-Que in Paragould is an important stop for any food lover. It's not just a great place to grab a pulled pork sandwich or a hearty breakfast, it's a time capsule for the Greene County town. The oversized restaurant is often full, and on its walls you'll find images from Paragould's earliest days.

The other location is Couch's Log Cabin Bar-B-Q. Run by Steve Horne, this location southeast of Jonesboro has been going strong since 1984.

Fortunately for Jonesboro residents, there's still good barbecue to be found at another classic: Demo's Smokehouse. The barn-style restaurant smells like a good July afternoon outdoors—lots of sweet smoke and wood. It's the place in the area for true St. Louis–style ribs, and the smoked chickens are excellent. Demo's does a lot of catering around the area these days, and its sweet peppery main sauce is divine.

GINA'S PLACE, JONESBORO

One of the best local lunch spots is out of sight of the roadway. Gina's Place is tucked into the far side of Fountain Square off Highland, and it's been offering amazing sandwiches and plate lunches since 1983. Many call it by its previous name, Ann's.

A slice of peanut butter pie at Gina's Place in Jonesboro. *Kat Robinson*.

Ann Maynard and Glen McKay started the restaurant up some thirty years ago. Their daughter Gina worked there through high school but left to go to business school and start her career. Jonesboro eventually pulled her back, and she returned to the restaurant. When her mom decided to retire in September 1997, Gina and her brother, Vernon, suggested they buy the place and take it over, but Ann said no. She didn't want them to go through the strife of running the restaurant.

The restaurant had a buyer, and Ann walked away, but that buyer came back a month later and said it wasn't going to work. Gina and Vernon McKay bought it and took it over immediately.

Vernon eventually left, but Gina is still making it work. A few years ago, she decided it was about time the restaurant bore her name, and so Ann's Restaurant became Gina's Place. Not much else has changed. Baked pork chops are offered every Wednesday, coconut cream pie on Thursday and salmon patties on Friday. A second generation of families now comes in for a bite on a regular basis.

The secret item for breakfast lovers is, I kid you not, called Garbage: two eggs, hashbrowns, onions, peppers, tomato, jalapeños, cheese and a choice of meat all grilled up together. A hot mess, but a good one.

Salmon Patties

1 16-ounce can or sealed package salmon
2 large eggs, beaten
1 small onion, finely grated
2 tablespoons fresh parsley, minced
Ground black pepper, to taste
1–1½ cups fine, dry breadcrumbs
3 tablespoons butter

Flake salmon with a fork. Beat together grated onion, parsley and pepper. Mix with salmon. Add enough bread crumbs, about ½ to ¾ cup, to make thick enough to shape into 12 small patties. Roll patties in ½ cup bread crumbs. In a large heavy skillet, over low heat, melt 2 tablespoons of butter; add patties. Fry patties slowly on one side; add remaining butter, turn patties and fry until brown on the other side. Serves 6.

Munchy's Specialty Sandwiches in Jonesboro. *Grav Weldon.*

MUNCHY'S SPECIALTY SANDWICHES, JONESBORO

Every college town has a local college eatery. For Jonesboro, it's Munchy's Specialty Sandwiches. Though a small chain was attempted decades ago, this original, slightly expanded shop is all that remains, serving sandwiches for a pretty low price to hungry college students and town residents.

Munchy's offers pretty traditional sandwiches. There is one called the BBQ & You that's barbecue sauce over roast beef, and there's Roger's Delight, which features roast beef, turkey, American and Monterrey jack cheeses dressed with lettuce, tomato and onion. One thing's for certain—if you're a Red Wolf (or, for older Arkansas State University alumni, Indian), this is a haven for nostalgia.

PRESLEY'S DRIVE IN, JONESBORO

In a different time, Presley's Drive In was a place of summer. Started by Harold and Hettie Mae Presley back in the early 1970s, it passed first to their son Terry Presley and then to Gary McGill. It's a fine dairy diner that has now served western Jonesboro for more than forty years. The décor has always been simple dairy diner, with a nod to a distant relative born in Tupelo.

My boyfriend and I lived a half mile west of Gee Street in the late 1990s, and we'd gather up laundry twice a month and head over to the Magic Touch for a laundry derby. Once the first round of loads were in on a Monday afternoon, I'd walk over to Presley's and pick up brown derbies for us both.

Gee Street was much different then. All sorts of restaurants lined the streets, like the Milky Way Drive In and Grandpa's, along with the old grocery store, flea markets and low-rent motels. In the summer, it was whitewashed and ancient and out of time.

When Grav and I went back to see Presley's in March 2014, we found nothing the same on Gee Street. The grocery store that still took stamps was now a Hays Supermarket, and the little diners and lunch counters were, all of them, absorbed into the past—except Presley's, which was almost untouched. There it stood, recently painted, depictions of menu items painted on the windows and a full house of customers. I wanted a brown derby, but I was denied. On this particular visit, the ice cream machine was out.

It made no difference. While Grav scarfed his half of a particularly excellent Reuben sandwich, lovingly butter-toasted on both sides, I picked at my offered Oreo cake (light and fluffy!) and at my memories, too—of those laundry days, of very hot summer days when I decided like a fool to take the dog for a walk, puffing the breath out of my lungs while standing at the outside counter with Jeffro, my Great Dane. Not only would I get my burger and fries and a big vanilla Coke, but they'd always offer Jeffro a vanilla cone, and it'd be gone in a swallow.

It's hard to believe that more than fifteen years have passed since I moved away, and yet this place is still here. That's partly thanks to David Stallings, who purchased the restaurant back in October 2012, not long after Gary's health got a little touchy. The menu hasn't changed a whole lot—there are still burgers, fries, shakes and the like, and breakfast and good plate lunches, too.

In fact, many of those more unusual dishes remain on the menu, like the Pizza Steak (a traditional Arkansas Delta pizza burger) and the Spanish Burger (with taco sauce). Other dishes could have been taken straight out of my *Tie Dye Travel* adventures—like the fried cheeseburger and the grilled cheese cheeseburger (the Excaliburger from the Ozark Café, seen on the back of *Classic Eateries of the Ozarks and Arkansas River Valley*).

There's something new that's recently shown up on the restaurant's Facebook page. Presley's now offers a competition burger called the King. It's seven pounds—four pounds of beef, a pound of bacon, plus toppings and bun, that come up to seven pounds total. You can buy it for $25 ($20 on Thursdays), and if you eat it by yourself in an hour, it's not only free but

The Fish Boat was started back in 1976 and is today run by Don and Kathy Stiles. It's known for not just catfish but also ribs, crab cakes and a famed strawberry cake. *Grav Weldon*.

Ron's Catfish, on the west side of Jonesboro past where Gee Street runs into Dan Avenue, is best known for its oversized buffet, which features catfish, hush puppies, crawfish, frog legs, shrimp, chicken and a dizzying array of desserts single-serve—including carrot and red velvet cakes, coconut and chocolate meringue pies, pecan pie, sweet potato pie, brownies and ice cream. *Grav Weldon*.

Presley's will also give you $100. From what I've seen, no one's managed to get that Benjamin Franklin yet.

Presley's has served Jonesboro for more than forty years, and if Stallings can keep ahold of it, it could go another forty.

Next time I go, I hope they have the brown derby again. I think, if it's summer, I'll sit outside on a curb stop and remember the traffic that used to pass on Gee Street.

SUE'S KITCHEN, JONESBORO

Sue's Kitchen closed in 1994, a year before I came to the city the first time. Situated in the Church Street Station building, it was the dominion of Sue Robinson Williams, who had been catering in the area since 1967. Williams started the restaurant in 1985 and had stayed with it for nearly a decade before turning back to catering with Expressly Sue's Catering. She and her son John ran that business until 2005. He took a few restaurant management jobs in the interim, but in August 2010, John Williams decided to reopen the restaurant in his mother's name in a downtown building that has served as a post office, a courthouse annex and a jail over its lifespan. The cavernous main floor of the building is mostly open, with dainty tables and large windows. The menu is very much teahouse meets burger joint, with a nice selection of sandwiches, specials and salads. And on Saturday, there's a brunch.

Hollywood horror movie star Vincent Price once begged for the recipe for Sue's famed peanut butter pie. Her decadently pink lemonade pie has become a recent fan favorite.

FRONT PAGE CAFÉ, JONESBORO

I'm not a big fan of having rolls thrown at my head. But some folks are, which is why restaurants such as Lambert's Café in Sikeston, Missouri, became so popular. Jonesboro has its own version in the Front Page Café. I used to love sitting in the old location on Caraway over by Barnhill's and passing around veggies family style to the folks at my table. I knew to make an agreement with the waitstaff early on—tips were contingent on me not getting crumbs in my hair from thrown rolls. Yes, that actually happened. Once.

Mike Felts opened the original restaurant along Caraway Road back in 1984 in the old Fat City Grill location. It was moved out to the bypass in 2001. The restaurant burned in 2008, but eight months later it once again opened. Current owner Mickey Felts (Mike's brother) made sure the restoration was complete, even the newspaper pages and sports memorabilia that line the walls were salvaged. He's also taken the opportunity to brighten up the menu with more items.

Still, there are pass-arounds like fried okra, beans, carrots and corn at lunch and dinner. And fortunately for those who haven't had their coffee, the biscuits are delivered on a plate at breakfast, rather than by air.

Lazzari Italian Oven, Jonesboro

The fact that my favorite restaurant in Jonesboro is Lazzari Italian Oven is no secret. It's the first one I ever dined at there. I stopped in at Lazzari Italian Oven after what I thought was my disastrous "I'm sorry, I know nothing about TV" job interview at KAIT in September 1995. I commiserated with my boyfriend over a Mista salad and a plate of pasta, and by the time we got to the tiramisu I had resigned myself to not getting the job.

Well, that was something. I did get the job after all and spent most of the next three years working as a television producer and getting to know the Upper Delta.

Lazzari Italian Oven opened up in 1994, a new venture from the folks that ran the Galley, a popular local fish restaurant. In fact, Lazzari is Italian for "galley," a fact I didn't know until I started researching this book. The eatery moved into a former Western Sizzlin' on South Caraway Road. It's not too fancy, but it is nicely decorated. Waiters come to the table and write their name on the white butcher paper overlay with crayons (being able to sign one's name upside down seems to be a condition of employment), light a candle and bring the best Italianesque bread in the world with olive oil, pepper and whipped butter.

Those sesame-encrusted salty top loaves are addictive, and they don't stop coming until you're done. The Mista salad—a sweet, soaked salad with pepperoncinis, tomatoes, olives, artichoke hearts, onions and lettuce with cheese—is equally habit-forming. And Lazzari's asiago cream sauce paired with sundried tomatoes in a number of dishes, such as the cannelloni and the beef ravioli, is stupendous.

Now, some great place where you can still have a great salad, entrée and dessert for two people for twenty dollars should be able to tough it out with no problem, right? When Olive Garden opened across town with its private license and reputation for endless salad, there was some concern that it would chase Lazzari out of town. Nope. The restaurant's homemade sauces and reasonable prices have kept it afloat. And if you really want wine with your meal, you can bring it in yourself.

TRUMANN

Southeast of Jonesboro, U.S. Highway 63 runs as an expressway unimpeded through its meeting with Interstate 55, south of Turrell. There's been word for years that the stretch will be renamed Interstate 555, but even though signs are in place, we probably won't see that happen in my lifetime. See, one of the rules of being an interstate is that you can't have farmers crossing those lanes getting from one field to another. So it's either build overpasses and underpasses for tractors to traverse those roadways, or not be an interstate.

Past the last Jonesboro exit, the highway quickly falls into a long flat plain of farmland that stretches out in every direction. In the fall, travel can be treacherous as farmers burn off fallow fields (a practice that may soon be eliminated).

Trumann started off as a lumber camp along the Frisco rail line. Back then, the area's position in the sunken lands (a region that includes part of Poinsett, Green and Craighead Counties to the east of Crowley's Ridge that sank during the New Madrid Earthquake in 1811) encouraged forest growth, and the heavily wooded areas were perfect for harvest. The town of Mosher was established in 1896, only to have its name changed to Weona in 1902 (there's a town named Weona about fifteen miles away today) and then to Trumann in 1904, which was named, you guessed it, after a railroad executive, in this case one from New York who never visited.

The craziest thing that ever happened in Trumann occurred during World War I. At the time, communities all across the country were being encouraged to out-patriot each other by fundraising with Liberty Loan drives. Residents got so caught up in the fervor that those who didn't contribute (or didn't give enough) were shamed. One day during a particularly enthusiastic rally, town fathers publicly whipped two men who refused to support the drive. The crowd surged through the streets, and a local merchant was pulled from his store by ladies and whipped while his store was painted yellow. Egged on by adrenaline, the "loose women" of Trumann were rounded up and thrown in the slough. They were hauled out by the proper ladies of the community, lashed and put on a train out of town.

Trumann flourished in the twentieth century as a Singer town; all that timber made good wood for making sewing machine cabinets. Industry still finds a home there, as do many Jonesboro workers who seek the amenities of a small town.

There are several great places to eat in Trumann, including the earlier mentioned Couch's Log Cabin Bar-B-Q. Another barbecue joint, Al's Barbecue, lies along Arkansas Highway 463 in town. The restaurant dates back to 1969, and it could just as easily be called Norma's. The grandmotherly figure who greets you when you walk in the door is Norma, and she expertly calls every order to the kitchen, just as she's done for more than three decades.

The barbecue at Al's is okay, but what the place is known for are hand-pulled chicken tenders and a proprietary ranch dressing that's made at the store. Locals know the best bargain is to order the buffet so they can enjoy as many of those marvelous hand-battered strips as they'd like.

Next door to Al's, you'll find Hightower Tastee Freeze, a classic dairy diner known for great burgers and fries that's been around since 1980.

Jerry's Steakhouse opened in 1981, and I'm going to be honest with you, it's a real dive. But it has the best steak in all of northeast Arkansas. Jerry Pillow took a Sears backyard grill, fitted it into a fireplace and created an

Al's Barbecue in Trumann. *Grav Weldon.*

altar to flame-broiling behind a bar in a one-room saloon. It didn't take long for word to get out about the fantastic grilled steaks and burgers he could conjure from his makeshift apparatus. A legend was born.

Jerry retired in 2000, and his son Tracy and daughter-in-law Kellie took over. They added sandwiches, including the Jerry's Signature Steak Sandwich, and put in a large commercial grill. Three years later, they bought the place next door and opened up a wall for more dining.

Any Arkansas State University student on a budget will tell you the best way to treat the person you're trying to woo is to take them to Jerry's on a Thursday night for the Sweetheart Special. That's a large ribeye and a small ribeye with potatoes and salad for about thirty dollars (the same deal with sirloin is twenty-one dollars). Flame-kissed steaks will keep Jerry's going for years to come.

MARKED TREE

The Southern Tenant Farmers Museum enhances knowledge and understanding of tenant farming and agricultural labor movements in the Mississippi River Delta. It opened in 2006 in the historic Mitchell-East Building in Tyronza. During the 1930s, the building housed the dry cleaning business of H.L. Mitchell and the service station of Clay East, two of the organizers of the Southern Tenant Farmers Union. It served as the unofficial headquarters for the union from 1934 until its offices were moved to Memphis for safety a year and a half later. Learn more at stfm.astate.edu.

Farther down U.S. Highway 63 sits Marked Tree, which itself sits between the Saint Francis and Little Rivers. That may not be unusual, but this is: the rivers run different directions. Marked Tree is named for an old oak tree on the Little River that used to have a big M on it.

After World War II, a new fad quickly caught on everywhere across the United States—a run of little restaurants little more than quick-serve kitchens that operated out of windows and served items such as burgers, ice cream and fries. These drive-ins became popular, not just because of the lack of a need for waitstaff or someone to clean a dining room but also for their quick preparation of food items. They also spread quickly thanks to the car culture that followed the war, as an era of prosperity allowed more Americans to own their own vehicles. Dining in said vehicle became a novelty, and the drive-in catered to that aesthetic.

Walker's Dairy Freeze actually started out in 1951, serving up burgers and specialty drinks such as the Purple Cow to a community that fell in love with the place. Its current owner, Evelyn Walker, purchased the restaurant in 1981 and has changed little about it. In fact, the original sign sits out front—completely unreadable.

Evelyn still works at the little stand, with its two windows and a drive-thru, making hand-dipped shakes and brown derbies. She prides herself on a menu where even the pickiest eater will find something to eat. Alongside burgers and fries and tots, you'll find fried chicken gizzards, fried shrimp, catfish, onion rings, barbecue sandwiches and what's considered the best pizza burger in the area.

A pizza burger is similar to a steak sandwich but includes marinara and mozzarella in its below-the-crust construction. Traditionally served on a bun with Miracle Whip (instead of mayo) and lettuce, it's a longtime favorite for drive-in lovers across the Delta.

DYESS COLONY AND JOHNNY CASH

These lands between Marked Tree, Tyronza and the Mississippi River have had their share of good and bad. They were also home to one of the greatest singers in American music.

J.R. Cash was born in a little town called Kingsland in Arkansas's Timberland Region. He was three years old when his parents, Ray and Carrie Cash, moved to Dyess as part of the Dyess Colony Resettlement Area in 1935. The young boy grew

A Painted House, a novel written by attorney-turned-author John Grisham, is celebrated at a home in Lepanto constructed for the Hallmark Hall of Fame movie of the same name. Tours are available upon request. More information is available at LepantoAR.com.

up, went to church there and even suffered his first loss when his beloved brother Jack died following a sawmill accident in 1944.

The boyhood home of Johnny Cash at the historic Dyess colony. *Kat Robinson.*

Cash took the name Johnny when he went into the air force in 1950. He would later tell audiences how many of his songs were influenced by his time at home, including "Five Feet High and Rising." He would go on to be inducted into the Country Music, Rock 'N' Roll and Gospel Music Halls of Fame.

In August 2014, Historic Dyess Colony: Boyhood Home of Johnny Cash was opened. The attraction includes both the restored home itself and the old Dyess Administration Building, which records the history of the colony and holds many old Cash family items, including Johnny Cash's air force uniform and Boy Scout book. Learn more at dyesscash.astate.edu.

9

THE GREAT RIVER ROAD, NORTH

Blytheville is a shrinking town, thanks to the end of Eaker Air Force Base. It's never had it really good, unless you count the great lumber years after the famous Chicago fire. It lies near the epicenter of the 1811 New Madrid Earthquake, was once home to one of the state's largest thriving Jewish populations (now mostly relocated to Memphis and Little Rock) and has risen and fallen on the back of cotton harvests.

The town reached a zenith in the 1970s, with a population of around twenty-five thousand. But with the closing of Eaker in 1991, it has radically shrunk and is now home to just fifteen thousand. Blytheville is the birthplace of Michael Utley of Jimmy Buffett's famed Coral Reefer Band, Hays Supermarkets and pig meat sandwiches.

Okay, the last one there might not be 100 percent correct—heaven knows, even the ancient Romans had pork—but the particular style of pit-smoked pork butts is the signature of Blytheville's eight establishments serving barbecue.

DIXIE PIG, BLYTHEVILLE

The most notorious is, without a doubt, Dixie Pig—the joint that started it all.

The original Dixie Pig began as the famed Rustic Inn in 1923. It sells "old-fashioned southern pit sandwiches" with vinegar slaw. It has never closed. The Halsell family that runs the place trace their lineage back to Ernest Halsell,

The famed Dixie Pig in Blytheville. *Grav Weldon.*

the proprietor of the Rustic Inn, a log cabin that sat beside U.S. Highway 61 and served "foods you like," as the sign out front said. The Rustic Inn was a AAA, Duncan Hines recommended eatery and the first stop you had to make heading north on the trek from Memphis to St. Louis. (The postcard view of the Rustic Inn is featured on the cover of this book.)

Ninety years of refining sauce and smoke have paid off. The Halsells don't use spice or rub on those pork butts. Instead, they're seasoned only with the smoke from charcoal and hickory for hours, until they fall apart. The sandwiches are a pile of meat and cabbage slaw on a bun. The sauce is thin, peppery and hotter than you think it will be. The combination is addictive.

BLYTHEVILLE'S BARBECUE

Many claim Dixie Pig is the best; others swear by Yank's Famous Barbecue, others still by Penn Barbecue. I was a pretty big fan of Benny Bob's, mostly for the incredible smoked chicken, but that restaurant burned in early 2014. Kream Kastle is almost always mentioned as a favorite; opened in an old Sonic-style drive-in, it's served up pork sandwiches and burgers for nearly fifty years.

But if you're headed through Blytheville and you have some time, look this one up: in the parking lot of the flagship Hays Supermarket (I'll get to that in a minute), you'll find a little red trailer where you can get yourself a pig meat sandwich, freshly smoked and piping hot. The trailer has been there a decade or more and it gets plenty of clientele. They call it Old Hays, but I don't think it actually has a name. I have seen a grown man let grease dribble down his chin and onto his shirt without a care in the world, biting into one of those pig meat sandwiches.

Kream Kastle in Blytheville. *Gray Weldon*.

Penn Barbecue in Blytheville. *Gray Weldon*.

HAYS SUPERMARKET

The grocery store one tends to visit is shaped by the region you are in. Kroger covers most of Arkansas, while Albertson's dot the southwestern portion of the state. Harps is expanding, and Memphis-created Piggly Wiggly has a store or two left.

But in the Delta, it's Hays Supermarkets. The first location was opened in 1935 by Russell and Mae Hays. Russell Hays came by his grocery background naturally. His uncle was A.W. Hays, who had joined brother-in-law David King and sister Mattie Hays King in the King Mercantile enterprise that had spread across eastern Oklahoma and even into Van Buren, Arkansas, in the 1910s and '20s. A.W. Hays thought it was his personal responsibility to tend to the needs and educations of the children of both David King (who died in 1931) and Hays's own brother William. Russell, William's son, was the first to benefit.

That first Hays store, opened in Blytheville (a half block from the current location), was a general mercantile that carried all sorts of dry goods. The operation's own website notes that a disgruntled competitor told a salesman once, "At Hays, you're likely to find a smoked ham and silk dress hanging on the same rack!"

A second store was opened on the square in Hayti, Missouri, in 1948. In the late 1950s, the store evolved into Hays Supermarket, and today there are a dozen Hays locations.

JERI-LIN'S DONUTS, BLYTHEVILLE

Amidst all of Blytheville's barbecue, a single shining pastry shop stands out. Jeri-Lin's Donuts has served the city since August 1969. The creation of Jerry and Linda Musser (the Jeri and Lin in the name), the shop is a perennial favorite.

The couple originally moved to Blytheville in 1967, with friends George and Shirley Miller, to close down one Montgomery Ward store and open another. During Jerry's college years, he had worked at a bakery and dreamed of opening a mom-and-pop doughnut shop. It didn't take long for the couple to find an old building to set up shop. Ironically, it was in a small grocery store that had once belong to the Hays family and then the Hoffsteter folks. At the time, the Musser kids were just ten and six years old, and they grew up at Jeri-Lin's.

The shop became a community hub. Students from the high school would swarm the place before school and at lunchtime. Airmen stationed at the base were instructed to pick up enough for everyone in their squadron. People would cram into the tiny shop, a rite of dining in the town.

The couple was active in the community. Jerry Musser got to be known for being able to portray Santa Claus very well, and he appeared for more than twenty years in parades and at functions as the jolly old elf—to the point that

Jeri-Lin's Donuts started out in 1967 in an old grocery store once owned by the Hays family. Today, it's located in a former bowling alley. *Grav Weldon.*

his own grandchildren called him "Grandpa Santa." Both Jerry and Linda gave what they had, whether it was Linda offering free doughnuts for functions or Jerry driving a boat and pulling kids that wanted to go water skiing, they were there.

Unfortunately, the little building they started in wore out. Jerry Musser passed away at the age of seventy-five, just before the move three blocks to the new Tenth Street location in the old bowling alley across from Blytheville High. Today, Linda Messer runs the restaurant with Melissa Grant, who has made doughnuts at the shop for more than twenty years. At the old location, there's a little park where the old building once stood, and a sign pointing the way to those fresh, light pastries.

Locals enjoy fantastic cinnamon rolls, chocolate-covered donuts and big fluffy doughnuts with the filling spooned on top. They also know the secret of the Smush—go in and order a Smush and you'll get a caramel doughnut smushed on top of a cinnamon roll.

WILSON CAFÉ, WILSON

U.S. Highway 61 winds its way down to West Memphis from the northeast corner of the state, running parallel to Interstate 55. It passes through Osceola and its Cotton Inn Restaurant.

Lee Wilson's visit to England inspired Wilson's downtown Tudor architecture, including that of the Wilson Café. *Grav Weldon.*

Farther south, you'll find new ideas, fresh produce and preserved traditions in a tiny Tudor town a mile from the Mississippi. Locals will tell you that there's always been a tavern in the heart of Wilson. It's had many names and many proprietors, but the little dining spot on the town square has been going for more than one hundred years. The Wilson Café operates in that building today and carries on the tradition.

The little town along the Great River Road is named after R.E. Lee Wilson, who traded his late father's cleared farmland for timberland, then held onto the property and started what would eventually become a company town. He built a sawmill, and by 1886, there was also a company store and residences. Around the turn of the century, the tavern opened its doors for the first time.

In 1925, R.E. Lee Wilson's similarly named son returned from his honeymoon in England with a vision of what the town of Wilson should look like. The new buildings that went up during this time had a strong Tudor influence, and older buildings were retrofitted to match this new wood-and-brick style. Every building took on this veneer, including the local department store, post office, bank, gas station and grocery store.

What's beyond the doors of the cottage-style Wilson Café is a surprisingly updated menu with a locavore commitment, thanks to chef Joe Cartwright. Locals pack the place out Tuesday through Saturday for lunch or brunch, joined by others who come from Memphis, Jonesboro and even farther away.

We stopped in on a January afternoon. The main room was packed and noisy. I saw salads and sandwiches and lots of hot beverages (it was a very windy day, probably forty degrees when we arrived). Conversations abounded.

The main room is large, but there are also other rooms—a private front room with a large table and chandelier and a lounge toward the back with its own entrance. Along one wall, there's a full station of glassware. Along another is a wait station and a line of paintings by local artist Norwood Creech.

Chef Joe's specials for the day included a catfish po' boy, a smoked turkey and provolone sandwich, sweet potato pie and sweet potato soup. The soup is hot, fragrant and reminiscent of Sunday after Christmas, a steamy concoction of pureed sweet potato nurtured with nutmeg, cinnamon and other spices. My pan-seared Mississippi catfish, served with roasted root vegetables and the Nice Little Salad, was the best catfish I have ever had in my life—buttery, perfectly seared and seasoned, light but warming, with a careful hand to the Creole spicing scattered on its top and utterly marvelous.

One of my dining companions that day was John Faulkner with the Lawrence Group, which hopes to revitalize and refocus Wilson. He shared the story of how Joe, formerly of the Elegant Farmer in Memphis, came to the place. Turns out, John would call about to different restaurants in Memphis looking for a suitable candidate willing to pull up roots and set up shop in a tiny burg. And one day, Chef Mac Edwards answered the phone. He suggested asking Joe, a young man who's spent a good portion of his life in the Arkansas Delta. Joe agreed, moved to Wilson and on December 20, 2014, served up his first menu at the Wilson Café. He uses locally grown produce—some of which comes from a large plot across U.S. Highway 61 and the railroad tracks, some of which comes from the farmers' market that's being nurtured to take over the old Lee Wilson and Company building.

Joe's tour de force that day wasn't the marvelous chocolate chess pie or sweet potato pie offered with hand-whipped cream, but his signature doughnut bread pudding, made from eggs, milk and torn pieces of doughnut, topped simply with real whipped cream and surrounded by a drizzle of crème anglaise. And if you're not hungry now, what's wrong with you?

The thirty-two-year-old Memphis-born culinarian was raised in West Memphis, attended Arkansas State University as a music education major and got his start cooking at Lazzari Italian Oven. He worked his way up through the Memphis food scene with stints at the Mesquite Chop House and Spindini. Wilson Café could be considered a bit of a stretch or a bit of a challenge. Joe seems to be the sort of guy who enjoys a good challenge. Creating a fine dining establishment in a remote Arkansas Delta town should fit the bill.

BIG JOHN'S SHAKE SHACK, MARION

A caramel apple pie at Big John's Shake Shack in Marion. *Grav Weldon.*

Loretta and John Tacker started up a Tastee Freeze in Marion back in 1977. They soon renamed it the Shake Shack (John's sister Sherry had a Shake Shack in Tyronza), but it eventually came to be known as Big John's Shake Shack because John got, well, big. And it's no wonder: John had a one-half pound burger he came up with called the Big John, and it's on the menu right next to country ham sandwiches, catfish, chicken, barbecue and milkshakes. Frankly, Big John's Shake Shack served just about everything.

John died in 2005, but Loretta Tacker keeps it going. She works alongside her children and even one of her grandsons in this three-generation eatery. Because the restaurant opened the year Elvis Presley died, he never ate at Big John's Shake Shack. But he's well represented with all sorts of memorabilia. Who knows about the place? Well, famed actor Gene Hackman, for one; former Arkansas governor Mike Huckabee, for two. But it's the regular customers like the kids from the local elementary school down the street who are truly prized customers.

The restaurant's become well known for pies—long before *Arkansas Pie: A Delicious Slice of the Natural State* came out, folks would come over from Memphis to enjoy both pies in a pan and handpies (fried pies). The hot fudge pie recipe came from Jeannie Oher and was an instant hit in the 1980s. Loretta says her friend Butch convinced her to do fried pies back in the 1990s. She makes pecan pies from the pecans dropped by the trees in her own yard. She's been making lattice-topped pies since her grandmother showed her how when she was a kid. And everywhere in the Shake Shack you'll find pies—fried pies in a case by the register with peach, cherry, chocolate, apple and caramel apple in wedges; whole pies in standing cases; and icebox pies in the freezers.

Part Three

THE CORRIDOR

10

U.S. HIGHWAY 70 AND INTERSTATE 40

PANCHO'S MEXICAN RESTAURANT, WEST MEMPHIS

When I give talks or sit in on seminars around the state and the subject of cheese dip comes up, I am invariably asked by someone in the audience to verify that Pancho's Mexican Restaurant is the birthplace of cheese dip. And I have to disappoint them.

Cheese dip, while an Arkansas original, wasn't created and first sold in West Memphis. Thanks to the groundbreaking research of Nick Rogers and his fine documentary *In Queso Fever*, we now know that Blackie Donnelly created the first true cheese dip after a trip to Mexico in the 1940s, and that he first served it at Mexico Chiquito when he moved his restaurant from Hot Springs to Prothro Junction (now a part of North Little Rock).

Pancho's Mexican Restaurant opened its doors in 1956. Morris Berger and his son Louis Jack Berger went on a trip to Mexico that year to celebrate Louis Jack's graduation from high school. They were so inspired by that trip that they returned to West Memphis and opened Pancho's in a structure they built with packed dirt floors and a live tree in the center. That first location was destroyed nine months later by a misguided eighteen-wheeler. The Bergers tore down the old Plantation Inn and built Pancho's Mexican Restaurant in its place. Brenda O'Brien (sister to Louis Jack and daughter of Morris) now runs the show.

Today there are three Pancho's—two in Memphis and the remaining location in West Memphis. Little has changed in fifty-eight years. The interior still resembles a cave, the taco dressing is addictive and you still get your cheese dip

The early days of Pancho's Mexican Restaurant. *Courtesy Pancho's Mexican Restaurant.*

delivered to the table at room temperature. That's no mistake—dip is always served less than hot—it clings to tortilla chips and mixes well with the house salsa.

Pancho's cold dip does make it easier to sell. For several years, the eponymous cheese dip has been available at retailers all over Arkansas and just across the border in Oklahoma, Missouri, Tennessee and Mississippi. It's usually found in either the deli or dairy sections (it requires refrigeration), and in recent years, a white cheese dip, salsa and the restaurant's famed hot sauce has joined it in stores. I'm excited about the recent addition of the sweet and tangy dressing; a dabble of that cilantro-and-mustard liquid on lettuce with a little tomato is enough for a refreshing starter or snack.

Not in Arkansas? Pancho's ships. Yes, you'll miss out on the atmosphere and the lover's lane of booths in the dark interior, but at least you can enjoy your cheese dip in your skivvies if you want to.

WILLIAM'S BAR-B-Q, WEST MEMPHIS

William Maxwell's joint is located on Fourteenth Street in West Memphis, behind businesses that line Broadway (U.S. Highway 70). In the heydays

William's Bar-B-Q in West Memphis. *Gray Weldon.*

of the 1950s and '60s, it was here that the blues took root. Memphis may lay claim to being the home of this particular American music style, but its birthplace was firmly entrenched in Arkansas Delta soil. Three blocks from where William's Bar-B-Q sits today, Howlin' Wolf slept at an Eleventh Street boarding house. Legendary radio station KWEM, first on-the-air in 1947, sat down the street at Broadway and Second Streets. A little farther away, B.B. King began entertaining crowds at the Square Deal Café, referred to as Miss Annie's Place, on South Sixteenth Street.

Blues and barbecue grew up together here. Maxwell worked as a cobbler at the Main Street Shoe Store in 1961; by 1963 he had been allowed to start selling barbecue, and in 1968, he opened up his own joint on Eighth Street. Over the years it stayed busy, thanks to all the traffic coming over from Memphis. Back then, Beale Street was all about jazz, and the clubs closed at midnight, but in West Memphis they'd stay open all night—and all week—long.

The barbecue back then was sandwiches, and it remains so to this day. Few realize that ribs didn't really take off until the 1970s, and fewer still note the existence of barbecue on this western side of the Mississippi, thanks to fantastic marketing and expansion of the famed Memphis barbecue-style. William's Bar-B-Q manages to hang on where urban decay has swallowed so much around its current Fourteenth Street location. Relocated in 1998, it's not apparent to the folks who pull off Interstate 40 or Interstate 55 looking for a way to get around the never-ending road construction. For those who do find it, some are overwhelmed when they step through the black-barred doorway and enter the dining room packed with old television sets (few of which appear to be operational).

Invariably, I go when I come through town, and I find out they're out of barbecue. That's not to say there isn't still a good reason to go. After all, William's also has what could be considered the best burger in the area. Still, I know that look on the faces of the individuals sitting outside the front door on a pretty day when I pull in at 11:30 a.m.: the 'cue is gone, might as well come back tomorrow.

When it can be found, though, it is marvelous. William's doesn't waste time on ribs or plate dinners. Here, the menu is all about sandwiches—sloppy, huge Boston butt sandwiches where the meat is crowned not only with a firm sauce but also a finely chopped slaw.

HOWARD'S DO-NUTS, WEST MEMPHIS

Gregory Howard's famed Howard's Do-Nuts chain is a Memphis institution, but it started at a West Memphis Harlow's Honey Fluff Donuts way back in 1971. Gregory changed the name in 1982, when the Harlow's franchise chain went out of business. His son David started a Memphis branch in the 1980s, and it's grown from there.

The elder Howard was flying a plane back in 1996, when the aircraft went down, killing the doughnut store owner. The original shop continues under son David. David's brother John and brother-in-law Daniel Zarella own several locations around the Memphis area.

A tall sign bearing the old Howard's Do-Nut sign is easy to spot from Interstate 40, and not much has changed inside. The doughnuts are magnificent and marvelously varied. Customers rant and rave over German chocolate and red velvet varieties, cream doughnuts with the filling on top, incredible Hawaiian pineapple fritters that are duplicated nowhere else and legendary cinnamon doughnuts. There are still Bible verses written on the

Howard's Do-Nuts in West Memphis. *Gray Weldon.*

whiteboard on the back wall and the admonition of a cartoon Howard on the production line window that clearly states "Prices subject to change according to customer's attitude."

U.S. HIGHWAY 70

The Lee Highway, the Broadway of America, that grand band of asphalt that once tied the coasts together along its southern belly, slashes across Arkansas as U.S. Highway 70. It began with an 1824 order to create a military road from Memphis to Little Rock, crossing the ridge and fording the Saint Francis River. Years later, it would parallel a railbed connecting the two cities. Once designated Arkansas Highway A-1, the stretch through the Delta was claimed in the name of Confederate General Robert E. Lee in a push to tie together an alternate route for the Lincoln Highway (incidentally, U.S. Highway 62, which became part of the Lincoln route, passes through northwest Arkansas). At one point, it ran all the way to Los Angeles; it was later superceded. Today it ends in Arizona.

In eastern Arkansas, Interstate 40 parallels its entire length, never more than a few miles away. With the completion of the Hernando De Soto Bridge to Memphis in 1973, most travelers chose the quicker road with its limited interruptions over the two-lane road and its bevy of businesses.

UNCLE JOHN'S ITALIAN RESTAURANT, CRAWFORDSVILLE

If you were to head out of West Memphis on Interstate 40, you'd quickly come to an exit for Highway 79, which, if headed south, will take you through some of the most strikingly beautiful flat river lands where little cell signal comes through, past Greasy Corner (where there really should be a classic restaurant, but there's not) and through Hughes to Marianna, where we started this journey on page 22. But if you were to double back along the highway and turn north onto Arkansas Highway 50, going under the interstate and due north, you'd come to Crawfordsville.

You'd pass it swiftly if you were on Highway 64—that roadway has long bypassed the tiny town, where few businesses manage to survive. But if you miss it one way or the other, you'd miss one of the state's biggest secrets.

That place is Uncle John's—an improbably comfortable Italian restaurant that manages to survive on word of mouth. Indeed, I wouldn't have found it had it not been for the recommendation of fellow writer Rex Nelson, who insisted I had to try it and consider it for this book.

Fellow writer Kim Williams helped make it happen on a Wednesday afternoon when the rain threatened to blow in. We made it there after the

Uncle John's in Crawfordsville. *Grav Weldon.*

lunch rush. There was one lone diner, a cook in the back and a waitress who insisted I had to have fried mushrooms. I did, and they were good.

Uncle John's was originally opened in 1984 by John and Lucille Marconi. John was a good farmer and a good cook, but when farming went to crock in the early 1980s, he started cooking more, first for family and friends and then for the community. The couple bought the restaurant from Lucille's sister, who was about to close it down. The Marconis started serving up the family's Italian recipes to hungry eaters, along with non-Italian eats such as hamburgers and cold sandwiches and, on Fridays, catfish. John didn't believe in advertising. He thought that if the food was good, people would come and share the word. He was right.

The Marconis raised seven children. Some went into the priesthood and some went on to start families of their own. The youngest, Michael Marconi, stayed, and when John passed away in 1994, Michael took over the running of the restaurant.

The menu is rather vast—and includes steaks, ribs, barbecue, toasted ravioli and spaghetti and a lasagna I could go back for again and again. One thing is certain—the dessert you really must have when you go is the bread pudding. It's far different from anything else you're going to find. See, Lucille Marconi didn't care for traditional bread pudding, especially how it was served in New Orleans, because it invariably contained raisins. The texture was different, too.

The Marconis tried a lot of things, but one night when they were out of other sorts of breads, they resorted to hamburger buns—and that was just the thing. The softer buns absorbed the egg, milk, sugar and bourbon custard to create an amalgamated pudding both delicate and assuredly firm enough to slice. It's topped with a marvelous bourbon sauce (though, if you ask nicely, you can have yours topped with lemon sauce instead). It's always heated, and that warm fulfillment at the end of a meal is about enough to put you to sleep; though, with no hotels nearby and considering the great distance you'd have to go to get anywhere with a bed, you'd best get yourself a driver.

Uncle John's isn't just neat because of what it serves; it's also unusually gorgeous inside. Sure, the main room is pretty standard restaurant, with a counter at the back tacked all over with business cards, but in the second room there's a fantastic mural that dominates an entire wall. It's a painting by local artist Joann Bloodworth, who envisioned the restaurant set in the hills of Tuscany. I'm told most of the residents of Crawfordsville are depicted in the scene.

KITCHEN'S CORNER CAFÉ, HETH

There's not a whole lot that can be said about the flat piece of ground where U.S. Highway 70 meets with U.S. Highway 79 just south of Interstate 40, other than it's a four-way intersection you cross to head south to the tiny town of Heth. Oh, and there's Kitchen's.

That building deserves interest. It's been standing since 1905, and it's housed a grocery non-stop for more than one hundred years since. One side

Kitchen's Corner Café in Heth. *Grav Weldon.*

used to be a liquor store, and the front part used to be a gas station; even today, it's also a bait shop and restaurant. What it is is a place you should stop and get yourself some breakfast.

For the past seven years, it's been known as Kitchen's Corner Café Grill and Deli (and Bait Shop, by one sign). Before that, it was run by most of the same folks as Boles' Grocery. Seems one of the Kitchen's boys married into the Boles clan some time back. Boles' Grocery goes back to the sixties.

The place is a mish-mash of every type of backroads gathering place you'll find in the Delta, with a meat counter, apothecary-style cabinetry, beverages, supplies and sundries. There's also an open kitchen with a bar for diners. The grill starts up at 5:00 a.m. and keeps going until 5:00 p.m. Everything's made right there in front of Heaven and all creation.

As can be expected for a blue-collar workingman sort of establishment, meals are on the large side. What's served? "Slammin!" barbecue made on-site, daily lunch specials, philly cheesesteaks and deli sandwiches and a half pound burger. Get the idea?

Breakfast is a must with good thick sausage-roux gravy made in a skillet over home-baked biscuits, plate-sized pancakes drizzled onto a well-seasoned grill and flat envelope-fold omelets that swamp platters. They'll even throw a thick slice of bologna on the grill to go with your toast.

There aren't a whole lot of places you can find yourself in a casual conversation with a duck hunter, a tractor-riding soybean farmer and a suited Memphis businessman at the same time, but this is one of them.

THE OLE SAWMILL CAFÉ, FORREST CITY

The Ole Sawmill Café goes back seventy-five years to a woman by the name of Liberty Bell. Lib, as they called her, started selling burgers for a nickel from the Street Car Café all the way back in 1939.

She was one tough cookie. When meat shortages caused her to need to raise the price to seven cents, one of her customers confronted her and complained. She got in his face and said "I'm sorry, I meant they're now a *dime!*"

Her husband Tommy served in World War II, and while he was overseas he'd send money home, which Lib used to purchase railway dining cars to add to the ends of her streetcar. Tommy came back and worked alongside her, and one day bought a barber shop in town. Lib opened the Liberty Bell in the space next door.

Her grandson Tom Stewmon tells me his mother worked there, too. "The last restaurant [my grandmother] owned was twenty-four-hours. And once she worked thirty-six hours straight. My mother was her relief. When she got there, Grandma Lib didn't say a word; she just picked up her purse and cut out."

Lib tried to sell the café several times to her employees—they thought they could run the business like she had, but every time she tried that, she ended up buying it back. Tom told me Lib always put an ad in the paper later that would simply say "I'm back—Lib Stewmon."

Interstate 40 came through Arkansas in the 1960s and '70s, and Lib could see what was coming. She worked with her son's brother-in-law Gene—who just happened to be a New York-trained chef—to build a new Liberty Bell close

The Ole Sawmill Café in Forrest City. *Grav Weldon.*

to where it was going through. Tom started his culinary career at the new restaurant and moved on to various food and beverage operations.

Lib finally did sell the Liberty Bell and retire, but the restaurant was destined to end up in family hands. Bill and Sara Stewmon purchased it and renamed it the Ole Sawmill Café, and it operates to this day.

Forrest City is the only city in the world that doubles the letter "r." It's named for Civil War Confederate general Nathan Bedford Forrest—the inspiration for the name of the lead character in the movie *Forrest Gump*.

Tom Stewmon was kind enough to share Grandma Lib's famed biscuit pudding recipe with me.

Biscuit Pudding for Supper

5 eggs
3 cups sugar
2 teaspoons vanilla
4 cups whole milk
1 stick (½ cup) butter
1½ cans (total of 18 ounces) evaporated milk
¼ teaspoon nutmeg
¼ teaspoon cinnamon
1 9"x11" pan leftover buttermilk biscuits or equivalent

Combine all ingredients and place in baking dish; cover with biscuits. Bake for 18 to 20 minutes at 350 degrees. Do not overbake. Remove from oven while dish is still jiggly.

Sauce:
1 stick (½ cup) butter
½ cup sugar
1 teaspoon vanilla
1 tablespoon heavy cornstarch
1 cup water

Simmer in saucepan until it thickens, then spoon over biscuit pudding.

Phillips Fish Market, Forrest City

Inez Phillips was a force of nature. Even now, nearly a decade and a half after her death, people in Marianna and Forrest City talk about her.

She and her husband, Richard, had a grocery store in Marianna for decades. When it came time to retire, they sold the store to their son and his wife, but Inez missed talking with folks and cooking for them. So in March 1980, she and Richard opened the Phillips Fish Market on Broadway in Forrest City.

"She didn't like the idea of being retired," her grandson Aron told me:

> *She was a busybody. The idea of the restaurant was to serve cooked fish and sell raw fish, something she could do where she could meet people. The place became so popular that within a few years she couldn't do it alone,*

Phillips Fish Market in Forrest City. *Grav Weldon.*

so she got my dad to do it. Eventually she thought she'd retire again, but she still kept coming in and talked with people every day.

Rock 'N' Roll Hall of Fame member Al Green hails from Forrest City.

She told you exactly what she thought, but she wasn't mean about it. Every person who ever met her loved her, and people still talk about her to this day. People will come in and ask me about something or have stories to tell me about things that happened years ago.

Aron hadn't planned to go into the family business. He was a student at the University of Arkansas at Little Rock (UALR) when his father fell ill and sent for him. "My dad got sick and had me come home—and then eight years later I'm still there, so it's just destined to be. It's something I never wanted to do, but all roads led back to it."

Phillips Fish Market will probably move from its original location soon—Aron is eyeing a location on the east side of town, still on Broadway but closer to the interstate and to Crowley's Ridge Community College. The menu will remain the same. "We sell catfish and we sell buffalo—that's a pretty big fish for us. It's not my favorite thing, but I will eat it occasionally. We do barbecue and great hamburgers, and we sell crawfish. We have people who come all the way from Little Rock to get raw fish. There are so many people who lived in eastern Arkansas who moved away who come back just for the fish."

At the time of this writing, there's even a plan to franchise out to other Delta locations. Aron believes there's just as much of a connection between catfish and the Delta as there is between the land and its barbecue.

Catfish is just as iconic as barbecue—everybody still cares for fried catfish as much as barbecue. I mean, we are big, big barbecue people and big fish people. I will go anywhere and if I see fish I'm going to try it. Everybody has a different spin on it, just like barbecue, everyone has a different way to do barbecue and everyone cooks catfish differently and what we have has worked at our place for thirty-four years.

GENE'S BARBECUE, BRINKLEY

Lewis DePriest started up Sweet Pea's Pit BBQ in 1971. He sold the business to his older brother Gene in 1994. Since Gene's name went up on the sign, the restaurant has not closed for anything, not for Christmas or Thanksgiving or Easter or even when the place caught fire. Gene DePriest is determined to serve up good food every day he's on this Earth.

The red, white and blue–roofed restaurant is unmistakable, sitting along the main drag south of Interstate 40 in Brinkley. Inside, there's barbecue and catfish and chicken-fried steak, sandwiches and burgers, quail and country ham and, in the mornings, a breakfast that will stick to your ribs.

In the fall and winter months, the restaurant serves as a jumping-off point for dozens of duck hunters. After all, this is the Arkansas Grand Prairie, and Brinkley is just outside of the Big Woods.

The Big Woods of Arkansas covers 550,000 acres, the largest section of bottomland hardwood forest remaining in the Mississippi Delta north of Louisiana's Atchafalaya River. It covers public lands such as the Cache River and White River National Wildlife Refuges, the Dagmar, Black Swamp and Wattensaw Wildlife Management Areas and Benson Creek. It also includes land along the lower White River's tributaries, the Cache River and Bayou De View, the lower Arkansas River and the Mississippi River near the mouths of the Arkansas and White Rivers. That's a big hunk of land, and for the most part, it's pristine.

You hunt ducks on the Grand Prairie, but in the Big Woods you hunt with binoculars for the Lord God bird. See, Gene Sparling, an amateur naturalist from Hot Springs, was kayaking on Bayou De View one day in February 2004. He encountered an ivory-billed woodpecker, a species last confirmed to have been seen alive in 1944 in Louisiana and last believed heard in Cuba in the 1980s. To comply with the federal Endangered Species Act, the United States Fish and Wildlife Service formed a species recovery team to prepare a comprehensive recovery plan for the ivory-billed woodpecker. It's called the Lord God bird because that's the exclamation many have made when they've spotted that sucker.

Gene's has embraced that spotting, and though no one else has definitively found that fowl in the decade since the sighting, you'll see its depiction on the menu and on the pine wood walls.

There are mornings where every person in the place will be wearing camouflage. I've heard a dozen different international accents of new duck hunters brought to these tables by their guides for the "authentic Arkansas experience." My daughter's made a meal of nothing but catfish and tartar sauce here. I've devoured breakfast steaks and fried quail and even a buffalo burger at those wooden tabletops. But I have yet to be invited to come enjoy a wild game repast on a Sunday night.

See, there's your truly Arkansas experience. On Sunday evenings, Gene DePriest offers an invitation-only meal of wild game to the men who frequent the establishment. It started ages ago, when Gene's wife wouldn't let him cook his fried squirrel in the house. He'd take them up to the restaurant, cook them up and share them with his friends. A tradition was started.

I suspect—and of course, since I hear this secondhand, I am not the best nor most reliable narrator—that the offerings at these gatherings are seasonal, just as they'd be if you sat down at someone's home: river-caught catfish, crappie, bass and buffalo fish in the summer; squirrel, venison, elk and wild boar in the colder months. In Joe York's documentary *Gene's Back Room Wild Game Sunday Supper*, fried rabbit is shown alongside wild duck and greens. I hear Gene's own produce from his garden makes it through to the back room as well.

There's no cost for the repast; it's illegal in Arkansas to sell wild game in a restaurant. This may sound strange, but there have been plenty of instances in this state's history where that rule has been bent (the Gillett Coon Supper meat is trapped, not shot, and it's not in a restaurant).

How long will Gene's Barbecue go on? Gene is in his late seventies but shows no signs of quitting. Longtime dinner attendee (and the writer of the foreword of this book) Rex Nelson says he'll ask Gene if I can come one Sunday. I hope I have a chance to be an honorary guy for the evening before Gene gets tired of it, that's for dang sure.

> The halfway point on the Little Rock and Memphis Railroad Company's planned route became home to a group of workers that dubbed their campsite "Lick Skillet," since the meal prepared each evening after their labors were done was good enough to "lick the skillet." The town was later officially named after Robert Campbell Brinkley the president of that rail company.

DeValls Bluff

Past the Big Woods and the Dagmar Wildlife Management Area on U.S. Highway 70, you come to a small burg along the White River that was a stage for the Civil War. DeValls Bluff, named for Jacob S. DeVall, a merchant who was one of the first white settlers to the area, became a strategic river port.

Pies on the shelf at Ms. Lena's Pie Shop in DeValls Bluff. *Grav Weldon*.

When the Arkansas River was difficult to navigate, the White was usually still somewhat free and open. In 1863, Union forces occupied the little town, allowing troops coming upriver to deboard and hop on the Little Rock to Memphis Railroad to get to the capitol city. On the river's banks, Fort Lincoln was erected. No skirmishes happened here, but the town did expand to nearly two thousand people with the influx of Union soldiers, support staff and merchant vendors who came to the area to capitalize on the war.

Afterwards, the town shrank. Agriculture has always driven the little port. Today its claim to fame, aside from its Civil War significance, lies mainly in the barbecue and pies that come from a few locations in town.

The pies come from one of two places. One is a little trailer home on Arkansas Highway 33 just south of town, where Lena Barnhill started two generations ago. As mentioned in *Arkansas Pie: A Delicious Slice of the Natural State*, Ms. Lena's Pie Shop is now the dominion of Viv and Kim Barnhill, the second and third generations of the family. The fried pies are overstuffed masterpieces, and the whole pies are amazingly good themselves, but they're only available on Fridays and Saturdays.

To the west on U.S. Highway 70, there's a bicycle shed out back of a house where Mary Thomas began making pies for sale way back in 1977, all manners of egg custard and pineapple, meringue and sweet potato pies. You'll often catch a glimpse of someone trying to cross the highway to get over to the Family Pie Shop, a lost-in-time place that never changes.

Of course, those road-crossers are usually parked on the south side of the highway. Many park there for the specific reason of visiting the red-trimmed cream-colored building there; others are stopped by the unusual, distinctive scent that can sometimes be detected a mile down the road. The aroma laced with cinnamon or ginger is distinctive. Those aren't flavors most people associate with barbecue.

CRAIG BROTHERS CAFÉ, DEVALLS BLUFF

Lawrence Craig perfected his barbecue sauce while working on a drag boat on the Mississippi River. He was persuaded to bring his barbecue to customers, and so five years later he did, opening Craig Brothers Café in 1947 with his brothers Leslie and Wes Craig. Craig's, as it came to be known, served anyone with a dime in their pocket. The combination of Lawrence Craig's sauce with eight-hour hickory-smoked sliced pork ham became the flavor associated with DeValls Bluff. Sure, there are also

Craig Brothers Café in DeValls Bluff. *Grav Weldon.*

ribs, sliced beef, chicken and sausages, but it's the sloppy pork the joint is known for.

Lawrence Craig cited his wife, Alice, as the inspiration for the apple-infused slaw at the restaurant, as well as the person who got him to tune that sauce up to where it needed to be. He worked hard, even after she passed away in 1993, to keep on going. It paid off. When Bill Clinton was president, he hosted Lawrence and his son Robert in Washington, D.C. and celebrated this Delta treasure.

Lawrence Craig passed away in 2005, but Robert and his first cousin L.T. still run the place with their children. Like most good barbecue joints, Craig's isn't a looker. It's a little whitewashed building on the side of the highway with barely enough parking to spit at. Inside, the walls are simple paneling with strange woodland wallpaper strips, the menu's an ancient letter board on the wall and the clientele is varied. You order at the counter. You don't pay, you just tell whoever's taking your order what you want and you go sit down. She'll bring you whatever beverage you asked for and disappear in the back of the building, where aromas play in the atmosphere and pans clink.

One November Saturday back in 2010, Grav and I found ourselves looking for a bite to eat.

"Mild, medium or hot," my hostess asked when I called for a beef sandwich.

"Mild."

"Chips?"

"No, but I'll take as much iced tea as you'll drown me in."

She didn't take any lip from me, just glanced over at Grav.

"Um, beef," he stated.

"Mild, medium or hot?"

"Hot!" I gave him a weird look.

"Chips?"

"No, I'm good, but do you have Mountain Dew?"

She grunted and turned on her foot, waving with her hand toward the dining area. We took this as an indication we should sit.

A moment later she came sweeping through the doors with our beverages in hand, plunking them down on the table and attending to a guy who'd come in for a pickup order. She swept back into the kitchen, turned back out and started conversing with the guy right behind it. "You sure this is beef?"

"Yeah, I'm sure," he huffed.

"Well, which one's hot?"

He started to answer, but I missed that bit as she closed the door again. It wasn't thirty seconds later when she came sweeping back through the door, with our sandwiches wrapped in wax paper on little Styrofoam plates, evaporating after her delivery.

They were messy—very wet with the sauce and the coleslaw. I was afraid to turn mine over for fear of disintegration. They were almost identical in appearance. The hot sandwich was darker and smelled more of Tabasco and black pepper.

One bite told me a lot. Instead of a chopped beef, this was thinly sliced smoked ham, just thick enough to require teeth but not tough. It came in three layers tucked up underneath a pile of sweet slaw and a bun.

The sauce, though—you know, I know people who swear by this sauce, who come from states over to pick up a gallon when they're around (it's twenty dollars a gallon, in case you're wondering). And it is indeed a sauce that would be hard to duplicate. Craig's sauce ditches the sweet of many regional barbecue joints for a mature, savory sauce spiked with notes of cinnamon and sorghum. I couldn't tell you for certain what it is, nor would I divulge that secret if I could, but it's meaty.

When we were about done with our sandwiches, our hostess came back out to us with our check, which we paid up at the table in cash, less than ten dollars to get us back on the road, including the tip.

MURRY'S RESTAURANT, HAZEN

For Little Rock food lovers, there have always been pilgrimages suggested due east. Whether Gene's or Craig's, Dondie's or Uncle John's, there's been a line drawn in the virtual sand of the food-writing world. Cross it, visit the ancients of our era, and one begins the true path toward the equivalent of culinary street cred.

The Holy Grail of those epic quests has for decades ended near Hazen. Olden Murry's kitchen talents have become the material of southern legend. Heralded by generations of food lovers, beloved by diners for more than half a century, the former riverboat cook's rambling association of tied-together rail cars near DeValls Bluff was ugly, unruly and absolutely perfect. Celebrated southern food writer John Edgerton called it "a rambling catacomb of interconnected coaches, trailers and pre-fabricated rooms." Old-time *Arkansas Gazette* writer Mike Trimble declared it to be "what appears at first glance to be a minor train derailment." I guess "a hot mess" really didn't cover it.

Murry's Restaurant near Hazen. *Grav Weldon.*

Murry had been in the United States Army Corps of Engineers, and he'd been mauled by a winch. He apparently drew disability, which caused him no small number of issues years later when someone happened to figure out (probably from reading Trimble's *Gazette* article) that Murry was able to get along just fine after all. That someone was a reporter who'd gone to work for the Social Security Administration in the Disability Determination Department. Said reporter filed suit. When confronted with having to pay back the government, Murry is believed to have told the government it could have the restaurant, since that was all he had. In the end, the Social Security Administration ended the payments and Murry got back to what he did best—cooking up marvelous vittles.

Born in 1921, Olden Murry managed eighty-one years on this earth. Along the way, his acolyte Stanley Young learned the secrets of perfectly battered onion rings, fried fish and quail. Stanley and his wife, Becky, have been running Murry's for seemingly ever now, and in the twenty-first century, its location is on the other size of Hazen, out in a field. It's still a pilgrimage, but a comfortable one.

Grav, Hunter and I made it our last stop on a long day of mid-Delta restaurant hunting one Saturday in March 2014. We came for the catfish, for the rumor of good bread and for bread pudding I was told was worth slapping my mama (not that she'd put up with that sort of crap from me).

Within the large room we discovered a welcoming, peaceful evening, where we could sit still instead of driving on, where my daughter and I could all but inhale an entire loaf of soft-crusted buttery bread. Knowing full well how often places known for good catfish often turn out hot, greasy messes, I didn't allow my expectations to rise. My heart soared when my plate of seafood reached the table and I was treated to fluffy, almost airy, catfish fillets with paper-thin batter.

Still, that didn't entertain me as much as watching the platter of fried quail delivered to Grav, complete with bowl of gravy. Here was a man who had already determined his favorite quail in the state, the Boston Mountain fried quail at the Red Barn in Fort Smith (now gone), confronted with an even more succulent example of the dish. Indeed, as he picked out rib bones, I could have cackled with glee.

That bread pudding was every bit as good as it was rumored to be, covered in a sauce of butter and angel drippings, er, rum sauce. Hunter and I sparred with spoons over every dribbling.

The restaurant doesn't serve alcohol, though there was a brown-bagged something-or-another on a table nearby. Murry's doesn't accept credit cards, either, but that doesn't keep it from the fame and accolades it so rightfully deserves.

NICK'S BAR-B-Q AND CATFISH, CARLISLE

The next stop heading into Little Rock is Carlisle, and if you're talking classic eats, you're talking about Nick's Bar-B-Q and Catfish. The big sprawling restaurant just off Interstate 40 is usually packed with cars, and it holds within its walls the particularly Arkansas trifecta of barbecue, cheese dip and pie.

Nick's Bar-B-Q and Catfish in Lonoke, opened in 1972 by E.C. Ferguson, has the trifecta of barbecue, cheese dip and pie covered. *Grav Weldon.*

Nick's wasn't the given name of the founder, nor was it his nickname. In fact, most folks called E.C. Ferguson "Cleo," which I am given to understand was his middle name. Ferguson got the pit smoking the first time in 1972, the year before I was born. All of the meat at Nick's is smoked on-site.

Cleo passed away two decades ago, but the place is still family run. His widow, Dorothy, is in her nineties and still making the rib rub and sauce. His grandson Clay Waliski runs the show these days, with help from Ferguson's sons Todd and Craig.

There's always a family of some sort dining on one side of the restaurant or another, and there's always some sort of pie on the counter—fried pies with coconut, individually wrapped pecan pies, you name it. And then there's the cheese dip. I've had to stop over to pick up cheese dip there for others closer to home who want some for their own consumption. Me? I'll have mine with fries while I'm waiting.

LONOKE

At Tidwell's Dairy Bar in Lonoke, the next city closer to Little Rock, fries naturally come with cheese dip, a tradition that dates back to, well, before the place was Tidwell's. The old dairy diner still serves just about every variety of dog, burger and sud you can imagine.

Lonoke itself deserves special mention. It's the site of the oldest state-owned warm water fisheries in the United States. The Joe Hogan Fish Hatchery, started in 1929 by the man of the same name, is overseen by the Arkansas Game and Fish Commission. Each year, it provides millions of fingerling bass, bream, catfish and crappie for the state's waterways.

Lonoke gets its name from a single old red oak that stood alone at the edge of the Arkansas Grand Prairie, way back in 1898. A major hub for baitfish production, Lonoke is today considered the Minnow Capital of the World.

NORTH OF 70—DES ARC AND DONDIE'S WHITE RIVER PRINCESS

The whitewashed riverboat alongside the White River in Des Arc has never set to the river beside it; it's not seaworthy and was never meant to float.

Dondie's White River Princess in Des Arc was built to look like a classic paddle-wheeler. *Grav Weldon.*

Yet the idea of this place has floated a dream and a lesson: if you have something good, keep ahold of it.

Dondie's White River Princess opened in the late 1980s, a catfish buffet concept restaurant created by Dondie Guess, a local entrepreneur with a big idea. The idea seemed sound enough: sell catfish from a fancy boat right next to a river known for its catfish. However, Dondie had some big dreams, and they involved a place that got a heck of a lot more traffic than little Des Arc could manage. He wanted to try his luck in Branson, so he offered his establishment for sale to Mike Skarda. Now, Mike wasn't a restaurateur, but he loved to grill, so he decided to give this a go.

That was back in 1990, maybe '91. Mike ran that buffet for a while, but he saw a need to expand the menu and added items—steaks, specialty seafood dishes, appetizers and pasta. He still kept the buffet going, though, selling catfish, frog legs, shrimp and mudbugs to a standard crowd every Thursday, Friday and Saturday night (and the first Sunday lunchtime of the month).

What happened to Dondie? He built a new boat right on the Highway 76 strip, and it quickly sank; not the boat, mind you, but the restaurant housed within. Discouraged, he sold the landboat to another owner and headed back to Des Arc, where he hoped to buy the White River Princess back.

Nothing doing. Mike told Dondie, "I'll sell you my farm, but I won't sell you the boat."

Today, Dondie has a car dealership and Dondie's White River Princess is still afloat, financially.

One Thursday night in April 2014, we made the drive from Little Rock. The heady scent of seasoning and smoke brought us through the doors, and we quickly found ourselves seated in a dining room with a view of the beautiful White River arch bridge. There were noises overhead as well as around us—the landboat has multiple service levels, all decked out with wooden tables on wooden floors and the sweetest waitresses you can imagine.

This trip, Hunter had spied the buffet on arrival and begged a shot at it. There she found not only fried catfish fillets and steaks but also hush puppies, corn nuggets, apple sticks, smoked ribs, chicken strips, fried shrimp, peel-and-eat shrimp and spicy boiled crawfish. For a five-year-old Arkansas girl, this was heaven, and she got extra helpings of these and beans, coleslaw, tomato chunks and pickle spears.

Grav spied the chalkboard special of a twenty-two-ounce cowboy steak for the bargain price of $15.95. After the salad of iceberg lettuce, tomatoes and blue cheese dressing and the cottony-soft brown bread served up with uber-sweet honey butter, the monstrosity was delivered to the table, a ribeye and rib combination that fell over the edge of the plate and dared Grav to consume its considerable span. It came with a baked potato the size of a shoe and a cursory bowl of vegetables. I had gone conservative and chosen the twelve-dollar lobster-stuffed shrimp dish, eight fat butterflied shrimp with a hearty dollop of a homemade lobster dressing atop each, astride buttered angel-hair pasta.

Alerted to the big camera Grav carried and then shot with in his kitchen, Mike Skarda came out to speak with us. He shared bits of the tale of how Dondie's came to be in his possession (a couple frequent customers provided the extra color for the story later) and about his clientele. A full 80 percent of diners come from somewhere else, including a bunch out of Mountain Home (three hours away) who make a regular trip down for Thursday night's dinner, overnight in Little Rock, shop there and return home. Dondie's wouldn't survive without the folks who come from afar, and Mike is thankful.

He's busy the other days of the week too. He's also the Prairie County judge! His daughter has become a sommelier, and his son-in-law's a Scotch taster. Those are some fabulous family connections.

Dondie's isn't just right down the street from anything, but it is worth the drive out to Des Arc to get some good vittles at a reasonable cost. I've heard the eighteen-ounce porterhouse is an experience, and I'm excited to try it on the next go-round. My suggestion is to go on a Thursday, because on Friday and Saturday nights a wait is almost a given.

11

U.S. HIGHWAY 165

The Arkansas Delta spans the state north to south along its eastern edge, with the Mississippi River as its eastern border. Its furthest westward encroachment ends, quite literally, at the steps of the Arkansas State Capitol. Built on the first rise from the flatlands within the walls of a temporary penitentiary, the Capitol Building was first opened in 1914. Within its basement, it houses its own classic restaurant.

There will be time later to talk about that establishment, and all of Greater Little Rock's classic eateries. The journey contained in this section of the book covers a span of restaurants along U.S. Highway 165 heading east from town, a highway that takes travelers from central Arkansas to Stuttgart (see pages 79–86).

The first of these, a block off 165 on Arkansas Highway 161, might be the most recommended and favored restaurant in the state. Its history traces back to 1917. Built over the bank of a bayou off the Arkansas River, it started life as a general mercantile store for the town of Scott. In 1984, its owners created an Arkansas icon.

COTHAM'S MERCANTILE, SCOTT

Of course, I am speaking of Cotham's Mercantile. Longtime general store, former military commissary and criminal lock-up, today it's a must-stop for food travelers.

Cotham's Mercantile in Scott. *Grav Weldon.*

The creation of this icon began with the addition of a single table for area farmers who wanted to sit down and enjoy their lunch, rather than purchasing a wax paper–wrapped bologna sandwich at the counter and eating it on the front porch. Word got around, and it was soon discovered by that amazing eatery-seeking class of Arkansawyer that so often roots out the great restaurants like pigs hunting truffles. Of course, I am speaking of politicians. Not just any politicians, but a couple Arkansas movers and shakers by the names of David Pryor and Bill Clinton.

Back then, the place was Lee Cotham's, and once Attorney General Pryor and Governor Clinton started frequenting the place, it took on the moniker "where the elite come to eat." Indeed, it wasn't long before the store was full of tables rather than merchandise; and those tables were full of folks rubbing elbows and placing those elbows on the table while two-handing the restaurant's famed seventeen-ounce Hub Cap Burger with a side of double-dipped oversized onion rings.

These days, Cotham's is a legendary stop on the trail to the southeast. It's been visited by President George Bush, Food Network's Rachel Ray and the Travel Channel's Adam Richman, who (erroneously) attempted to eat the state's biggest burger by consuming a Quad Hub Cap on *Man Vs. Food* (the state's largest burger at the time of this writing is the five-pound patty on the famed giant cheeseburger at Ed Walker's Drive In up in Fort Smith). When you go, don't limit yourself to the burger. Check out what's on the lunch special board, and be sure to try the Mississippi Mud Pie.

CHARLOTTE'S EATS AND SWEETS, KEO

A short distance farther down U.S. Highway 165 lies a little village called Keo. There's not much to it these days, just the largely popular Morris Antiques, a handful of shops and Charlotte's Eats and Sweets.

Charlotte Bowls didn't set off to start a restaurant. She was going to be a caterer. In 1993, she rented out the back of an old pharmacy and started cooking. The folks in Keo were grateful for a good spot to grab a bite to eat, and they encouraged Charlotte to expand her menu. Over the years, she took over more of the building, clearing out old furniture, cleaning top to bottom and finding chairs and tables to fill the space.

Today, lines form outside Charlotte's place each day half an hour before it opens, and there's always a wait. Locals order by phone and come to pick up their Keo Klassic and slice of pie. The pies really are remarkable. Her coconut meringue was named best in the south by *Southern Living* ages ago. I went on about her caramel meringue in *Arkansas Pie: A Delicious Slice of the Natural State*. What can I add? Well, the fresh fruit plate with your choice of

Charlotte Bowls (on the counter) with her staff at Charlotte's Eats and Sweets. *Restaurant historical photo.*

a scoop of tuna or chicken salad or cottage cheese is a gorgeous choice for a light lunch. The cakes are stunningly good if you miss out on pie, and the gobstoppingly creamy shakes are perhaps the most overlooked sweet on any Arkansas restaurant menu.

SPRADLIN'S DAIRY DELIGHT, ENGLAND

A little community east of Little Rock may be home to the place where the Frito chili pie was created. I kid you not. Back in 1957, a man by the name of Claude Spradlin decided to open a dairy bar in the town of England, mostly because there wasn't already one in town and it seemed like a good idea. Claude's wife had worked at one in her hometown, so he opened up Spradlin's Dairy Delight.

Back in the 1950s and '60s, the restaurant came to be known for three things—burgers, footlongs and the Frito chili pie. Claude charged a nickel for the Fritos and a dime for the chili, and it caught on. He eventually received notice from the Frito Lay Corporation, which sent him a letter thanking him for his contribution.

Claude's son, Claude Spradlin Jr., took the place over in 1973. The younger Spradlin has always been around the restaurant; it first opened when he was seven. He took over grill duties at the age of sixteen and says he may have cooked more hamburgers than any man in America over the past fifty years. At the age of sixty-four, he's still manning the grill and having a good time. He says he visits each day with his buddies and has some great regular customers. And he has no intention of retiring.

Claude Spradlin opened Spradlin's Dairy Delight in England in 1957. *Courtesy Claud Spradlin Jr.*

HARDIN FARMS & MARKET TOO, SCOTT

I mentioned back on page 62 that there was more to the story of the Hardins of Grady. The story is two-fold. In 2010, Randy Hardin moved to Scott to start another farm. Hardin Farms and Market Too is the next iteration of the Hardin family's agricultural bent, and son Josh Hardin has been instrumental in bringing in fresh produce for sale. The restaurant's also great for very smoky barbecue. I have been known to stop in and pick up a smoked chicken or two to take home.

It's Josh's older brother, though, who's waving the banner for Delta farmers most fervently. Jody Hardin's efforts can be considered one of the cornerstone moments for the birth of the Arkansas locavore movement. Born in 1967, he took up farming with his family as a teenager. He headed off to college after high school but returned in 1994 to save the farm. As I've heard him mention before, "The irony of the Delta is it's beautiful but so hard to survive in."

Jody has been seeking out every way he can to help fellow farmers. In 2005, he spearheaded a basket-a-month program to bring produce, eggs, milk and meat from farms to city dwellers. In 2008, he moved to North Little Rock and, under request from then-mayor Patrick Henry Hays, he started up the Certified Arkansas Farmers' Market, which requires its members to verify that they are the source of the products they sell. In 2010, he was one of the key elements in the opening of Argenta Market, the first grocery store in the area to specialize in local produce (the market closed in 2014).

Hardin will tell you, he just really wants to be a farmer. But there's something in his down-to-earth demeanor that makes him a natural salesman and leader. Bedecked with hat and clad in jeans and boots, he's become an icon.

His latest effort has been to help farmers in the Delta grow organic and sell produce to its low-income communities at reasonable prices. He spent ten years knocking on the door of Heifer International, pointing out the plight of struggling farmers here at home (the organization is best known for helping impoverished families in other countries by sending them cows, chickens and other animals to help communities, especially women, to become self-supporting and sufficient). Heifer responded, and the Seeds of Change Initiative, a campaign to build resilient local economies and end poverty through the extraordinary potential of locally produced food, was born (to learn more, please head to heifer.org).

Today, Hardin spends much of his time in a 5,600-square-foot Italian villa on sixty-three acres of rich pastoral land. In 2013, the city of North Little

Rock approached him and asked if he'd like to take over the aging Saint Joseph's Center of Arkansas. The former orphanage, built around 1910, was empty and available. Hardin jumped at the chance, working not only to secure funding for a new nonprofit hybrid farmer innovation center but also to transform the land around the building into an urban garden. At the time of this writing, he's busy terracing the hilltop on which Saint Joseph's Farm sits and is working to overturn the city's ban on raising goats.

He's also working on a buy-in program, where families put down money and receive food from Delta farmers throughout the year. The money helps keep those farmers afloat, along with grants Hardin has secured to help them move into organic production. Those families receive the bounty of fresh produce, and Arkansas comes that much closer to coming full circle, celebrating its own agricultural treasures.

Part Four

OUT OF THE DELTA

12

SEARCY

There's a stretch of land that lies between the Ozarks proper and the Delta, claimed sometimes by neither and sometimes by both, that harbors a small wedge of cities. Many of these are served by U.S. Highway 67—in Bald Knob, Newport, Walnut Ridge and Hoxie and all the way to Pocahontas, where the ridge comes right into town.

If you go southwest of Bald Knob following U.S. Highway 67, you come to Searcy. Surrounded to the north and west by a ridge but open to the Delta to the south and east, it's a gateway to Greers Ferry Lake and trout fishing on the Little Red River. Home to Harding University, its most popular export is likely Yarnell's Ice Cream, the only statewide ice cream manufacturer left in Arkansas.

It has its classic eateries, though it's rare that news of these great places are lauded outside of town. Of note, there's Barb's Bar-B-Q not far from downtown. Barb's doesn't do a lot of barbecue—its menu is packed with burgers and sandwiches—but the little barbecue that comes from its smoker is pork butt, and it's served on sandwiches with a tangy mustard-based coleslaw that makes the experience like no other.

Every community has a dairy diner of some sort, and in Searcy, it's been the Frozen Delite since the 1940s. Located on Benton Road, it's been serving chili cheeseburgers, fries and the like to generations of families. Of note, the shakes are more like concretes, necessitating a spoon or a little patience if you really want to try to suck a lump of ice cream up a straw.

Catfish lovers should head to Huckleberry's Catfish Buffet over on Eastline. It's not much of a place to look at, just one gigantic high-eaved room painted white and packed with tables; but there are always crowds. The catfish is good, the gumbo is better, but by far the best thing on Huckleberry's Catfish Buffet are the massive cinnamon rolls. And of course, being a buffet means you can have as many as you want, though, if you can eat more than two you are a better man than I.

Yarnell's Ice Cream

Open since 1932—with an asterisk—Yarnell's Ice Cream was a family tradition for seventy-nine years. Roy Yarnell bought the old Southwest Dairy and Dairyland brands in a bankruptcy sale. He; his wife, Hallie; and their son, Albert, had their work cut out for them. They knuckled down and made the business work. That meant not drawing a salary for the first several years of operation. But those five-gallon tubs of ice cream sold to drugstores and ice cream parlors counted up, and when Yarnell was able to buy his first refrigerated truck, business boomed.

Albert Yarnell served in World War II and came back into the company in 1948 with an idea at aiming the product for home sales to address the boom of young couples who could afford their own homes and refrigerators. Albert took over when his father died in 1974, and his son, Rogers Yarnell, came on board soon afterward. Together they expanded the brand past just its classic Premium Red line to meet the growing ice cream demand, adding Guilt Free and frozen yogurt lines as they came into vogue.

The fourth generation, Christine Yarnell, joined the company in 2001. She added yet more options, including a Pink Promise line that turned back receipts into donations to the Susan G. Komen Breast Foundation. All the while, the homegrown plant kept its place in downtown Searcy.

That is, until 2011, when one June day employees reported to work to find the gates closed. Without warning, the Yarnell family had ceased their role in the ice cream business. Within hours the word had spread, and the remaining cartons flew off the shelves across the state as ice cream lovers got ahold of the final cartons of Woo Pig Chewy, Ozark Black Walnut and other longtime favorites. Restaurants that had long proudly served the famed Arkansas brand were left scrambling without

Arkansas governor Mike Beebe tries the first spoonful of Yarnell's from spokesman Scoop after the company's restart. *Kat Robinson.*

a source for proprietary recipe ice cream that had founded a basis for numerous desserts.

But there was hope. That hope came in a bankruptcy sale a few months later. That November, Chicago-based Schulze & Burch Biscuit Company bought the company part and parcel and tracked down the recipes that were sold off in the interim. The company, which also makes Toaster Treats at another Searcy location, came in and cleaned the plant top to bottom and then got to refining the oversized Yarnell line. In April 2012, in a big celebration at the Arkansas State Capitol attended by lawmakers and Governor Mike Beebe, the new Yarnell's was rolled out—along with a new mascot named Scoop, a delivery guy with a sweet tooth.

Yarnell's continues to flourish under Schultze & Burch. Today, it offers nine Premium Red flavors (Homemade Chocolate, Real Vanilla, Homemade Vanilla, Cookies & Cream, Ozark Black Walnut, Homemade Strawberry, Butter Pecan, Rocky Road and Death by Chocolate) as well as three Guilt Free flavors and five frozen yogurts, and the brand is once again a source of hometown pride.

13

BATESVILLE

Hanging tight along the last major ridge of the Ozarks, Batesville lacks the flatland the Delta shares. I briefly touched on it in *Classic Eateries of the Ozarks and Arkansas River Valley*. It sees itself as the gateway to the Ozarks, but I believe it's just as valuable as a gateway to the Arkansas Delta. As you wind out of town on U.S. Highway 167 heading due south, the ridgy hills quickly give way to first rolling land and then the big flat of the Delta, right at Bald Knob.

It shouldn't be left short shrift with its collection of old restaurants.

FRED'S FISH HOUSE, BATESVILLE

Fred's Fish House is all about the catfish, just like its fellow similarly named location in Mountain Home. Situated in an old church, Fred's is known for ample portions and an unchanging quality of fish and hushpuppies. But its history goes back farther.

Fred Ward started his Fish House in Cord, a ways out of Batesville, back in 1991. He'd have his sons fish for fresh catfish right out of the family pond to serve up at the little café and grocery store he ran. Problem was, word got out about how good and fresh his fish was, his sons fished the pond dry and he had to start getting fish from other places.

In 1991, Fred moved the business to Batesville and turned it over to his son Randy. The popular location continued to turn out hot catfish, spicy brown beans, homemade dressing, hush puppies and what's considered to be one of Arkansas's best green tomato relishes—so good, the Wards had to start offering them for sale in jars at the register. Today, Randy's sons Cameron and Brandon are involved with the business, and it continues to thrive.

Fried Catfish

From the Arkansas Farm Bureau
"This recipe will feed a dozen or more people at your next home fish fry. The hot sauce/ milk marinade adds a nice piquant flavor to the catfish without making it spicy hot."
—Keith "Catfish" Sutton

6 pounds catfish steaks and/or fillets
3 3-ounce bottles Louisiana style hot sauce
12 cups milk
3 cups yellow cornmeal
1 cup flour
2 tablespoons salt
1½ teaspoons cayenne pepper
1½ teaspoons garlic powder
Peanut oil

Marinate catfish 1 to 2 hours in a mixture of hot sauce and milk. Remove fish and drain. Combine the dry ingredients in a large plastic bag. Add the fish a little at a time and shake to coat. Cook the fish in 2 inches of peanut oil in a deep fryer heated to 365 degrees. Fry until the thickest part of the fish flakes easily with a fork, about 5 to 6 minutes. Remove and drain on a paper towel. Repeat with remaining fish. Serves 12–15.

Green Tomato Relish

This condiment isn't something you just whip up. Instead, it's the true purpose of the marvelously tart green tomato. Clear some counter space and make up a year's supply—or share with people you like.

7 pounds green tomatoes, cut into 1-inch pieces
4 large yellow or white onions, sliced into 1-inch by ½-inch pieces

2 large red onions, sliced into 1-inch by ½-inch pieces
4 teaspoons canning salt
5 cups apple cider vinegar
4 cups sugar
2 tablespoons celery seed
2 teaspoons mustard seed

Combine tomatoes and onions. Fold in salt. Pour into a cheesecloth-lined colander and let stand for two hours. Discard the liquid. Bring vinegar, sugar, celery seed and mustard seed to boil in stockpot. Add tomatoes and onions. Reduce heat and simmer uncovered for 30 minutes or until thickened and sinuses are clear. Carefully ladle the hot mixture into 8 hot pint jars, leaving ½ inch at the top. Remove air bubbles and add more of the hot mixture until it's even with the top. Wipe the jar rim and carefully center lids on jars. Screw on bands until tight. Place the jars in pot covered with at least one inch of water and bring to a boil for 15 minutes. Remove from heat and let cool. Yield: 8 pints.

Triangle Café and Elizabeth's Restaurant and Catering

Atop the hill overlooking the town from the south, you'll find the Triangle Café. It's been there since before the roads around Batesville were paved, at the corner of U.S. Highway 65 and Arkansas Highway 14. It opened in the 1940s, but since the '90s it's been Lisa Palmer's place. Each day, breakfast and lunch are served at this festive little spot along Main Street, where regulars sit and nurse coffee over pancakes or whatever the plate lunch happens to be.

Downtown, you'll find Elizabeth's, a bright and airy spot along Main Street offering beautiful dainty foods such as splendid cold sandwiches and a pineapple boat of a fruit salad, along with the Four Star Salad. If you're like me and have a hard time deciding on a dinner, this one takes care of your curiosity, with matching scoops of tuna, shrimp and chicken salads over pasta salad with pickled okra.

JOSIE'S AT THE LOCKHOUSE

Finally, there's Josie's at the Lockhouse. Steve Carpenter owned the original Josie's in Waldenburg. The relatively small restaurant would be packed on weekend nights when Josie's was open, with folks wedging themselves in to get a shot at one of the eatery's famous steaks.

Steve was happy there, but when this property opened up in Batesville, it was a deal too good to miss. He purchased the structure, built in 2000 over a 1910 lock, and opened Josie's at the Lockhouse in 2004. The new restaurant overlooks the lock that allows traffic to climb up northwest toward the lakes that dot the White River. Steve added a deck, a perfect spot for summer evenings where one can watch the sun set. Inside, local paraphernalia, signs and fishing implements crowd the walls. You can see the sign that welcomes diners to Josie's on the front cover of this book.

Steve's dishes focus on prime Angus beef, just as they did back in Waldenburg. The restaurant also features a mean club sandwich, excellent cheese dip and an outstanding example of bread pudding. It's become so popular that country music star Mickey Gilley has had to drop in for a bite and a chance to perform.

As the sun sets over the White River, the story sets for this book, strewn across the Delta's long flat plain. It ends here at yet another crossroads, where the Ozarks beckon. Grav and I will start a new journey soon to cover the southern and western regions of the state, but for now, a clear evening on Josie's deck will do us both just fine.

AN INCOMPLETE LISTING OF CLASSIC RESTAURANTS IN THE ARKANSAS DELTA

Al's Barbecue
229 Arkansas Highway 463
Trumann, AR 72472
(870) 483-6396

Amish and Country Store
3040 U.S. Highway 65
Dermott, AR 71638
(870) 538-9990
Amishandcountrystore.com

Arnold's Catfish Place
2122 South Blake Street
Pine Bluff, AR 71603
(870) 536-1384

Bar-B-Q Barn
5500 Green County Road 628
Paragould, AR 72450
(870) 236-8999

Barb's Bar-B-Q
905 West Pleasure Avenue
Searcy, AR 72143
(501) 268-3418

Batten's Bakery
1735 Paragould Plaza
Paragould, AR 72450
(870) 236-7810
facebook.com/pages/Battens-Donuts-
and-Bakery/301766555113

Big Banjo
720 Highway 65 South
Dumas, AR 71639
(870) 382-2880

Big Banjo
4208 West 28th Avenue
Pine Bluff, AR 71603
(870) 879-3801

Big John's Shake Shack
409 Military Road
Marion, AR 72364
(870) 739-3943
Facebook.com/theshakeshack

Bonnie's Café
103 Front Street
Watson, AR 71674
(870) 644-3345

Bulldog Drive In
3614 Highway 367 North
Bald Knob, AR 72010
(501) 724-5195

Burger Shack
372 Sebastian Street
Helena–West Helena, AR 72390
(870) 572-2271

Catfish Island
5319 Arkansas Highway 1
Caldwell, AR 72322
(870) 633-1706

Charlotte's Eats and Sweets
290 Main Street
Keo, AR 72046
(501) 842-2123

Colby's Café and Catering
805 South Falls Boulevard
Wynne, AR 72396
(870) 238-3636
Colbyscafe.com

Colonial Steakhouse
111 West 8th Avenue
Pine Bluff, AR 71601
(870) 536-3488

Cotham's Mercantile
5301 Arkansas Highway 161
Scott, AR 72142
(501) 961-9284
Cothams.com

Cotton Inn Restaurant
4635 West Keiser Avenue
Osceola, AR 72370
(870) 622-5800

Couch's Bar-B-Q
2108 Linwood Drive
Paragould, AR 72450
(870) 236-7207

Couch's Log Cabin Bar-B-Q
405 Arkansas Highway 363
Trumann, AR 72742
(870) 483-2433

Country Cupboard
2842 U.S. Highway 165
Wilmot, AR 71676
(870) 473-5151

Country Kitchen
4322 Dollarway Road
White Hall, AR 71602
(870) 535-4767

The Cow Pen
5198 U.S. Highway 82
Lake Village, AR 71653
(870) 265-9992
TheCowPen.com

Craig Brothers Café
15 Walnut Street
DeValls Bluff, AR 72041
(870) 998-2616

Dairy King
205 Front Street
Portia, AR 72457
(870) 886-6301

Dairy Shack
7964 U.S. Highway 49
Waldenburg, AR 72475
(870) 579-2214

Demo's Barbecue & Smokehouse
1851 South Church Street
Jonesboro, AR 72401
(870) 935-6633

Appendix

Dixie Pig
701 North 6ᵗʰ Street
Blytheville, AR 72315
(870) 763-4636

Dog n Suds
319 East Kingshighway
Paragould, AR 72450
(870) 236-8511

Dondie's White River Princess
203 East Curran Street
Des Arc, AR 72040
(870) 256-3311

Elizabeth's Restaurant and Catering
2131 East Main Street
Batesville, AR 72501
(870) 698-0903

Family Pie Shop
U.S. Highway 70 W
DeValls Bluff, AR 72041
(870) 998-2279

Fred's Fish House
3777 Harrison Street
Batesville, AR 72501
(870) 793-2022
fredsfishhousebatesville.com

The Fish Boat
3905 East Nettleton Avenue
Jonesboro, AR 72401
(870) 910-4900

Front Page Café
2117 West Parker Road
Jonesboro, AR 72404
(870) 932-6343

Frozen Delite
2030 Benton Street
Searcy, AR 72143
(501) 268-4732

Gene's Barbecue
1107 Arkansas Highway 17
Brinkley, AR 72021
(870) 734-9965

Gina's Place
2005 East Highland, Suite 109
Jonesboro, AR 72401
(870) 910-3900
Eatatanns.com

Hall's BBQ
152 North Main Street
Dumas, AR 71639
(870) 382-4922

Hamburger Station
110 East Main Street
Paragould, AR 72450
(870) 239-9956
Facebook.com/HamburgerStation

Hardin Farms and Market Too
15235 U.S. Highway 165
Scott, AR 72142
(501) 961-1100
Hardinfarmsandmarket.com

Hickory House BBQ
128 U.S. Highway 64 W
Wynne, AR 72396
(870) 238-4041

Hightower Tastee Freeze
149 Highway 463 North
Trumann, AR 72472
(870) 483-2464

Ho Ho Chinese Restaurant
110 Barrow Hill Road
Forrest City, AR 72335
(870) 633-3888

House of Lee
125 U.S. Highway 65 North
Dumas, AR 71639
(870) 382-2388

Howard's Do-Nuts
1711 North Missouri Street
West Memphis, AR 72301
(870) 735-2046

Huckleberry's Catfish Buffet
2613 Eastline Road
Searcy, AR 72143
(501) 268-0192

The Hungry Man
2500 Arkansas Highway 367
Newport, AR 72112
(870) 523-8129
Facebook.com/HungryManRestaurant

Jeri-Lin's Donuts
840 North 10th Street
Blytheville, AR 72315
(870) 763-9679

Jerry's Steakhouse
424 Arkansas Highway 463
Trumann, AR 72472
(870) 483-1649
Jerryssteakhouse.com

Johnson's Freeze Inn and Fish House
329 U.S. Highway 64 East
Wynne, AR 72396
(870) 238-3371

Jones' Bar-B-Q Diner
219 West Louisiana
Marianna, AR 72360
(870) 295-3802
Facebook.com/JonesBarBQDiner

Josie's at the Lockhouse
50 Riverbank Road
Batesville, AR 72501
(870) 793-7000
Josiessteakhouse.com

Josie's Steakhouse
7964 U.S. Highway 49
Waldenburg, AR 72475
(870) 579-2277
facebook.com/josiessteakhouse
.atwaldenburg

Judy's Snack House
135 Greenwood Avenue
Lepanto, AR 72354
(870) 475-2340

Kelley Drug and Selections
300 North 2nd Street
McGehee, AR 71654
(870) 222-5071

Kelley's Restaurant
425 U.S. Highway 64
Wynne, AR 72396
(870) 238-2616

Kibb's Bar-B-Que
436 West 2nd Street
Stuttgart, AR 72160
(870) 673-4261

Kibb's Bar-B-Que #2
1400 South Blake Street
Pine Bluff, AR 71603
(870) 535-8400

Kibb's BBQ
1102 East Harrison Street
Stuttgart, AR 72160
(870) 673-2072

Kitchen's Corner Store and Café
26 Highway 79 South
Heth, AR 72346
(870) 735-5648

Kowloon Restaurant
1331 South Highway 65/82
Lake Village, AR 71653
(870) 265-3511

Kream Kastle
112 North Division Street
Blytheville, AR 72315
(870) 762-2366

Lavender's Barn
4703 Highway 65 South
Pine Bluff, AR 71601
(870) 536-2276

Lazzari Italian Oven
2230 South Caraway Road
Jonesboro, AR 72401
(870) 931-4700
Lazzariitalianrestaurant.com

Leon's Catfish & Shrimp
3801 Chapel Village
Pine Bluff, AR 71603
(870) 879-3150

Lotus Blossom Restaurant
1623 S Main Street
Stuttgart, AR 72160
(870) 673-4060

Lybrand's Bakery and Deli
2900 Hazel Street
Pine Bluff, AR 71603
(870) 534-4607
Lybrandsbakery.com

Lybrand's Bakery and Deli
6201 Dollarway Road
Pine Bluff, AR 71602
(870) 247-5498
Lybrandsbakery.com

Mel's Steakhouse
8610 North Cole
Harrisburg, AR 72432
(870) 578-5153
Facebook.com/MelsSteaksandCatering

Ms. Lena's Pies
2885 Arkansas Highway 33 South
DeValls Bluff, AR 72041
(870) 998-7217

Munchy's Specialty Sandwiches
1320 South Caraway Road
Jonesboro, AR 72401
(870) 932-5360
Facebook.com/Munchys

Murry's Restaurant
Highway 70 East
Hazen, AR 72064
(870) 255-3266

Nick's BBQ & Catfish
1012 South Bankhead Drive
Carlisle, AR 72024
(870) 552-3887
Nicksbq.com

Old Hickory Bar-B-Q
320 Southwest Texas Street
Hoxie, AR 72433
(870) 886-2004

Ole Sawmill Café
2299 North Washington Street
Forrest City, AR 72335
(870) 630-2299
Olesawmillcafe.com

APPENDIX

Omar's Steakhouse and 501 Club
2628 Phillips Drive
Jonesboro, AR 72401
(870) 972-6501
Omars501club.com

Pancho's Mexican Restaurant
3600 East Broadway Avenue
West Memphis, AR 72301
(870) 735-6466
PanchosCheeseDip.com

Parachute Inn
10 Sky Watch
Walnut Ridge, AR 72476
(870) 886-5918
Parachuteinnrestaurant.com

Parkview Restaurant
1615 West Main Street
Corning, AR 72422
(870) 857-6884

Pasquale's Tamales
1005 Little Rock Road
Helena–West Helena, AR 72342
(870) 338-3991
Sucktheshuck.com

Penn Barbecue
367 South Division Street
Blytheville, AR 72315
(870) 762-1593

Penny's Place
210 Van Buren Street (U.S. Highway 49)
Weiner, AR 72479
(870) 684-2260
Facebook.com/Penny10101

Phillips Fish Market
122 Turner Road
Forrest City, AR 72335
(870) 633-1799

Pic-Nic-Ker Drive In
646 West Waterman Street
Dumas, AR 71639
(870) 382-5091

The Pizza Den
513 Norhtwest Texas Street
Hoxie, AR 72433
(870) 886-7752
The-Pizza-Den.com

The Pizza Den
1803 U.S. Highway 67 S
Pocahontas, AR 72455
(870) 609-1923

Pleasant Plains Dairy Bar
7649 Batesville Boulevard
Pleasant Plains, AR 72568
(501) 345-2287

Polar Freeze
416 U.S. Highway 67 North
Walnut Ridge, AR 72476
(870) 886-9976

Presley's Drive In
917 South Gee Street
Jonesboro, AR 72401
(870) 932-7835

R.A. Pickens and Son Commissary
122 Pickens Road
Dumas, AR 71639
(870) 382-5266

Ray's Dairy Maid
5322 U.S. Highway 49
Barton, AR 72312
(870) 572-3060

Rhoda's Famous Hot Tamales
714 Saint Mary's Street
Lake Village, AR 71653
(870) 265-3108

APPENDIX

The Rice Paddy Motel and Restaurant
4379 U.S. Highway 165S
Gillett, AR 72055
(870) 548-2223

Ron's Catfish
3213 Dan Avenue
Jonesboro, AR 72401
(870) 930-9639
RonsCatfish.com

Skipper's Catfish and Hamburger Delight
1211 Falls Boulevard North
Wynne, AR 72396
(870) 238-2270

Smokehouse BBQ
601 Malcolm Avenue
Newport, AR 72112
(870) 217-0228

Sno White Dairy Bar
405 Main Street
Des Arc, AR 72040
(870) 256-3306

Sno-White Grill
310 East 5th Avenue
Pine Bluff, AR 71601
(870) 534-9811

Sportsman's Drive-In
805 North Porter Street
Stuttgart, AR 72160
(870) 673-7462

Spradlin's Dairy Delight
324 North Main Street
England, AR 72046
(501) 842-2341

Sue's Kitchen
524 South Church Street
Jonesboro, AR 72401
(870) 972-6000
SuesKitchenRestaurant.com

Taco Rio
1713 Southgate Plaza
Paragould, AR 72450
(870) 236-8307
facebook.com/tacorio72450

Taylor's Steakhouse
14201 Arkansas Highway 54
Dumas, AR 71639
(870) 382-5349

Terry's Café
201 South Pruett Street
Paragould, AR 72450
(870) 236-7845

The Triangle Café
3 Triangle Lane
Batesville, AR 72501
(870) 793-7330

Troy's Drive In
1024 South Jefferson Street
De Witt, AR 72042
(870) 946-1201

Uncle John's Italian Restaurant
5453 Main Street
Crawfordsville, AR 72327
(870) 823-5319

Walker's Dairy Freeze
10 U.S. Highway 63
Marked Tree, AR 72365
(870) 358-2508
WalkersDairyFreeze.com

Appendix

Who Dat's Cajun Restaurant
3209 Arkansas Highway 367
Bald Knob, AR 72010
(501) 724-6183

William's Bar-B-Q
106 South 14th Street
West Memphis, AR 72301
(870) 725-0979

Willy's Old Fashioned Hamburgers
300 East Speedway Street
Dermott, AR 71638
(870) 538-5090
facebook.com/willyshamburgers

Wilson Café
2 North Jefferson
Wilson, AR 72395
(870) 655-0222
eatatwilson.com

Woody's Bar-B-Q
5599 Arkansas Highway 14 East
Waldenburg, AR 72429
(870) 579-2251
BuyWoodysSauce.com

Yank's Famous Barbecue
213 East Main Street
Blytheville, AR 72315
(870) 762-2935

INDEX

INDEX

ABOUT THE AUTHOR

K at Robinson is a dedicated food and travel writer and lifelong Arkansawyer. She writes for a variety of publications and promotes Arkansas foodways and food history and is a research fellow with the Southern Food and Beverage Museum. Her award-winning blog, TieDyeTravels.com, features tales of her journeys and experiences in Arkansas, the American South and wherever she may roam. She lives with her daughter Hunter in Little Rock.

ABOUT THE PHOTOGRAPHER

G rav Weldon is a fine art photographer and digital artist currently living in Little Rock and working in the Ozarks and Mississippi River Delta—documenting the food, culture and history of the American South. His current works can be viewed at GravWeldon.com.

Check out these other titles:
Arkansas Pie: A Delicious Slice of the Natural State
Classic Eateries of the Ozarks and Arkansas River Valley
For more on this series, head to ClassicEateries.com or TieDyeTravels.com.